Wolves In Street Clothing
*How Animal Behavior Teaches Survival
in the Asphalt Jungle*

By
Kris Wilder &
Clint Hollingsworth

Illustrations by Clint Hollingsworth

Stickman Publications, Inc.
Burien, WA 98146

ISBN-13: 978-0692210888 (Stickman Publications, Inc.)

ISBN-10: 0692210881

Disclaimer

Information in this book is distributed "As Is," without warranty. Nothing in this document constitutes a legal opinion nor should any of its contents be treated as such. Neither the authors nor the publisher shall have any liability with respect to information contained herein. Further, neither the authors nor the publisher have any control over or assume any responsibility for websites or external resources referenced in this book.

Warning:. Neither the authors nor the publisher assumes any responsibility for the use or misuse of information contained in this book.

When it comes to martial arts, self-defense, and related topics, no text, no matter how well written, can substitute for professional, hands-on instruction. These materials should be used **for academic study only**.

Praise for "The Little Black Book of Violence"

"This wonderful book fills a necessary void of knowledge in the realm of martial science. I rate it at five out of five stars. Bravo!"
-- Jeffrey-Peter A.M. Hauck, J.D.

"Everyone with a pulse should read this book, but it's a must read for teenaged boys, who aren't likely to get this kind of a tutorial at home or school." -- William C. Dietz, bestselling author

"A very cool yet frightening perspective on violence; a book where the dreams of heroism and adventure are acted upon with proper fore-thought and intellect." -- Martina Sprague

"This book is an important work that all youth of any post-elementary school age should read or at least should have portions read to them (with the caution that the graphic nature of some of the words and illus-trations could be overwhelming to some adolescents). I like to call this book Scared Smart or at least Scared Thoughtful."
-- Michael F. Murphy, School Board Director

"A must read for any man or woman who is interested in learning not only how to defend oneself, but how to read other people's aggressions, and understand both the mental and physical aspects of violence."
- Staff Sgt. Bryan Hopkins, USMC

Praise for Wandering Ones: Ghost Wind

"A great book! Clint Hollingsworth is a great artist and storyteller. I al-ways wait impatiently for his online strips to come out and I never miss an opportunity to buy his books. You can tell Clint is a skilled outdoors person who is experienced in the way of the scout. The skills portrayed by the clan of the hawk in the books are wonderful and genuine. His characters and story lines are true and endearing. I can't wait for the next book!" - Xavier de la Foret

Acknowledgments

It is common to acknowledge the people that made a difference in your life, those that without knowing it contributed to this book.

First, our dads, both of whom spent hours in the outdoors and shared their knowledge with us in ways both serious and fun.

Tom Brown Jr. and Jon Young, both keen trackers and masters of wilderness awareness for their teaching and encouragement.

Our sensei, who guided, cajoled, pounded and molded us.

And a unique acknowledgment to the fields and woods of North Central Washington where the authors grew up. Simple lessons, silently taught in a direct manner.

On Wolves in Street Clothing

When Kris Wilder asked me to write a few words about the new book he co-authored with Clint Hollingsworth, I thought "why me?" Kris had listened, and as I began to listen to my own story it became evident why he asked me to write about it.

Growing up a physically small boy can be challenging. Growing up in a violent community, physically small, and a minority was just dangerous. Developing skills for survival was essential. Simple things I could do to avoid danger became; maxims to live by, such as "Don't go to the bathroom at school." reduced my exposure to violence. That single thing might seem simple to many, but that stacked on top of other protocol reduced my stress level where I could deal with other unexpected events that might come my way. That is where the skills come into play. I left home at age 15 and leaped into a sketchy world populated by boozers, users, losers, predators and criminals, mostly petty, all looking for easy prey.

In the 1980s, I came across Tom Brown's tracking school. Tom Brown's book The Tracker is now a classic, telling of his introduction to Native American wilderness survival. Learning the skills from him and his associate instructors I found a commonality between the environments that I had come from, the urban jungle where I had sharpened my survival skills and the wilds of the Pacific Northwest. I became acutely aware that is most instances a predator is just a predator no matter whether it stands on two feet or four feet, or swoops down from above talons splayed.

These days I am a personal security instructor, among other things, and although I live in a warm house in the suburbs, the woods call me whether the hills are covered in the summer sunshine or the winter snow. The environment is unforgiving by its, well…nature. It seems not a week goes by where the local news is not telling us about some hiker, or skier that is missing, lost, or just plain uncounted for. Add an extra layer of perdition to the already ambient environment and mistakes can threaten your life or in some instances cost you.

Our species has survived and flourished over thousands of years to become the number one predator of the planet. All this without the aid of ferocious claws, flesh tearing fangs or being physically the strongest or the largest creature out there. The difference is the brain. Homo sapiens' have flourished because of their ability think, learn, reason and out-think those that would eat them or otherwise do them harm.

Wolves in Street Clothing teaches folks to rekindle tools that are already in us -- already in our DNA -- and have been there for thousands of years, but our society had blunted them; muted them down. The book is not about strikes, kicks and blocks; it's not about grappling. This book is not about all the skills that take years to master and even more years to implement when you're stressed and adrenalized.

This book is about using the brain to 'not be there' when violence comes knocking, just as Sun Tsu taught us in "The Art of War" 5,000 years ago. Awareness/avoidance skills are a much better "bang for your buck" over martial arts training if safety from street violence is your goal. The skills taught in "Wolves" may very well prevent you from ever being forced to defend yourself on the streets. And as anyone experienced in street fighting knows, things seldom go as planned when it comes to street violence.

Wolves in Street Clothing is a book that needed to be written. It belongs in the library of every martial artist and every person that wants to take responsibility for his or her own personal security and that of their loved ones.

  - Ron Jarvis; Tracker, Outdoorsman, Self-Defense Instructor

Prologue

The Animal World Is Our Key To Understanding Predators

Human beings, who are almost unique in having the ability to learn from the experience of others, are also remarkable for their apparent disinclination to do so.

– Douglas Adams

Animals tell us how predators think, how they operate, what their methods are. Animals that are not predators will tell us, with their patterns and behaviors, how to live safely. While some animals are actually smart, most are at least clever. That is, they know what they are supposed to do, and they do it well and with little thought. As a friend from England, who rescues distressed dogs is fond of saying, "It's an open gate, and I am a dog. Why wouldn't I go through it?" The idea is that there might be something on the other side of the gate that I can eat, maybe fight, or, well, – the other F.

In today's industrial world, our awareness is dulled and atrophied by the safety that we have built around us. Often our greatest concern is getting a credit card bill paid on time to avoid the Draconian credit card penalty. If you want to see the animal brain at work, the next time you go to a fast food restaurant take a moment and throw a French fry on the pavement. If you have the same animals that we have here in the United States, a seagull or a crow will be on it immediately. If you do it twice, more birds will come. These birds will move fast, risk danger and steal from each another to get the food they need. From our vantage point, there is little honor in it. The fact is, honor doesn't exist in the animal world. The adage of the Law of the Jungle is, "kill or be killed." This is not necessarily an exaggeration. The world of the predator is one of alertness, always watching for the next opportunity. The world of the non-predator is also one of alertness, just with different intent and goals.

A story has it that retired fighter pilot and Brigadier General Ran Ronen of the Israeli Air Force had a dog fight that lasted eight and a half minutes – a phenomenally long time for a jet fighter duel, as most last only about thirty seconds. After chasing the enemy jet fighter through the desert canyons, Ronen hit the enemy jet with a short burst from his guns; he watched the enemy jet roll to its side and the fighter pilot ejected from his flaming jet. With rocket boosters blasting him from his burning jet, he was slammed into the wall of the canyon, killing him instantly. Ronen, in pursuit, watched the entire event. He had this to say; "I was happy that I was the one that landed safely. On the other hand, after such a fight of eight and a half minutes, the way it ended – leave aside that it is between enemies, leave that aside – as a fighter pilot, as a colleague - I felt he would have, you know, deserved to eject safely."

No such emotion enters the predator's mind. Honor, as we know it, does not exist. They do not think like you. The sooner you know this the better off you will be, and you will move through the world a little safer.

This book will examine, through the lens of the animal world, the mind of the predator and the mind of the hunted. Our goal is to shift your focus from the cerebellum and frontal cortex of your human brain down into the animal brain that we all possess, to see the world through the eyes of the predator that is innate in all of us.

Table of Contents

Introduction

Everybody leaves a trail; everybody signals their intentions.

"Change brings opportunity"

- Nido Kwiben

Well, that's not completely true. There are those rare people that do not leave a trail, but they are skilled in doing so and make an extraordinary effort to ensure that they don't leave a trail. There are also those few people who do not signal their intentions. These people often have some sort of psychological disposition that allows them to behave in a way that conceals their intention; for example, a psychopath, sociopath, or quite possibly an alpha predator who understands the concepts of surprise and violence and employs them adroitly.

In the February 16, 2012 issue of the New York Times, reporter Charles Duhigg illustrated how the store Target, through a complex matrix of shopping behavior, was able to identify that a young woman was pregnant before her parents knew. By identifying patterns of shopping behaviors, Target was able to find an abnormality, a break if you like, in normal shopping behavior. This break in the pattern was revealed to be a predictive indicator that this shopper was pregnant. Target has institutionalized this methodology and goes so far as to have what they call a "pregnancy prediction" score.

Just like in the physical world, your electronic transactions and online activity leave a trail. What you search for on Google, what you purchase with your credit card, etc. are all open knowledge to those who are willing to search the data or pay for it.

Anybody who has had any form of martial arts training will hear animals spoken of in the context of their art. If you're involved in Tai Chi or Kung-Fu you've no doubt heard of movements like, "White crane spreads its wings," or "Grasp the sparrow's tail". The entire system of Hung Gar is based on the two animals; the Tiger and the Crane. The system of karate that your two authors engage in has five animals that it emulates. Even in the Filipino arts there are techniques such as "Defang the snake". The metaphor is based on taking away the weapon (the fang) that is coming at you from the attacker's hand (the snake).

In his early years, Wilder lived on a ranch a good distance out of town. He tells this story. "One winter morning my father and I got into the family car and began the drive into town. As I looked out the window of the car I saw coyote tracks in the snow beside the road. I pointed out to my dad that I could see coyote tracks left in the couple of inches of the fresh snow. With a just quick glance toward where I was pointing, my father turned his attention back to driving and said, "It wasn't a coyote, it was a dog." I asked him how he could be so sure that it was a dog and not a coyote. Again without taking his eyes off the road, he said, "Coyotes don't light out like that. They don't make a straight line and usually not next to a road." As we drove into town he continued to tease out the explanation. He pointed out that the reason for this was based in the coyote's belly. Coyotes are always looking for their next meal, always seeking for any opportunity to feed. A straight line is about getting to a destination, not about hunting."

Patterns demonstrate behavior, and often the reason for that behavior. In many ways the lessons that we can learn from animal behavior are from those behaviors that are based on survival and making it to the next day.

In today's world, we are told that we need to be aware, and that this is the first and most important aspect of any form of self-defense. There are several problems with this idea. The first thing that you need to know is that the mind explains away the majority of the things you experience in your life. You don't need to be cognitively aware of absolutely everything in your surroundings.

The mind explains away the majority of your life. As an example, let us use a common chair. Once our brain is able to recognize a chair for what it is we don't have to test every chair to see if it is fit to hold our weight. We don't have to be aware of every chair, test every chair, or hold every chair as suspect. To prove this point, here is a test. Answer this simple question; please describe the last two chairs in which you have sat. You most likely cannot, because it is not important information anymore.

The human brain scans and throws away a lot of information that it receives every day. Indulgence us for just a moment. When you decide to send a picture to a friend on your computer you have many options of formats, for example, JPEG, and TIF. A JPEG basically goes through the picture and says, "there are a whole lot of dots here, and we don't need all of these dots, or pixels, of information; many of them are inconsequential to conveying the information needed." A JPEG file says to many of the pixels present in the picture you are sending, "Thanks for showing up, but go on home and we'll call you if we need you." At the other end of the spectrum is the TIF. A TIF has every piece of information lined up, ordered and accounted for. This is why when you want to send a picture of your latest adventure to your friends and family your system chokes on the high-content TIF and can't complete the sending of the picture. Yet the average person looking at these two files can't see a difference. This is because the brain is filling in the blanks. The brain is interested in the picture, not the pixels. The brain is seeking quick, swift pattern recognition and not detail – the patterns that you have adopted through your life, the patterns that allow you to swiftly recognize external patterns and make choices. These patterns serve you well, allowing you to get from point A to point B safely and efficiently.

Similarly, so has nature decided that some information is not necessary for your immediate survival; it has been experienced and cataloged, and therefore does not require your notice, or alert attention. Further, some information is difficult to assess, or hard to believe – it can lock down the brain as it attempts to process or to find similarity of experience in which to order and codify it. Your brain throws a lot of information away every second of every day. However it's our goal to show you how to use already existing information in the way that an animal uses its environmental information to bring you back in touch with the skills that you innately possess. These skills will allow you to see the patterns of your world in a new light, well, actually, an old light, and allow you to see, predict, and ultimately avoid conflict with a potential predator.

You're going to learn in broad sweeps how predators see the world. You are going to see how herd animals see the world. You will also learn how the human cerebral cortex and the sense of "I" do you few favors in regard to your survival, and in fact, can inhibit or even countermand successfully navigating a life-threatening situation.

Chapter One
Predator Encounter

"I have, indeed, no abhorrence of danger, except in its absolute effect – in terror."

- Edgar Allan Poe

We know there are predators in all environments. Wherever life can be found you can find a predator. However, living in the insulated world we've created, we usually forget that four-legged and two-legged creatures are out there that can mean us harm. These predators like it when we're oblivious to our surroundings, not paying attention, especially the imbedded predator.

Clint, one of the co-authors, was reminded of this possibility in the rainforests near the small town of North Bend in Washington State. Having spent the summer furthering his study with the Wilderness Awareness School (Wildernessawareness.org) he had adopted a remote spot in the forest along the Snoqualmie River where he would spend hours observing the creatures and plants living there. The object of this was to sit quietly by himself a few days a week, sometimes for hours, and simply observe the area, the movement of the animals and the interplay of the total environment. He would journal what he found, and then take that information back home to study and learn more from his field guide teachers.

As the animals of that area grew more accustomed to Clint's presence they became easier and easier to see and to track. They were less concerned with the potential threat that Clint presented. Clint also became more familiar with the local animals. Following their footprints he eventually began to recognize certain individuals by the nuances in each print. He had also begun a course in the study of bird alarm language. This ancient skill of knowing the alarms of various birds and their habits when giving alarm calls improved his three-dimensional awareness immensely. (Clint's mentor, Jon Young - http://jonyoung.org, has since written a book on this subject, *What the Robin Knows*.) This improvement of awareness kept Clint from having a nasty predator encounter.

As the summer progressed, Clint noticed that he was seeing less and less animal tracks, and sightings of deer and elk had dropped off to almost nil. Seeking as many tracks as he could, to practice his skills, the ongoing decrease of tracks increased his frustration. Even the most common of tracks, raccoon and muskrat, also dried up. After a little time, Clint began to feel as if he was the only mammal in the forest.

In the Pacific Northwest, the rivers are fueled by snow melt and the water level towards the end of August can reduce wild, rapid-filled rivers to tepid streams, easily crossed by wading or hopping from rock to rock. As the water dropped, Clint finally decided to leave his familiar turf and venture to the other side of the river in search of new tracks. What he found on the other side opened the first possibility in his mind that there might be more than non-threatening herbivores in the forest with him. The beach and trails of the far side of the river, away from Clint's familiar adopted woodland area, were covered with animal tracks. This was unusual, as the presence of the new houses on the immediately adjacent hillside would most likely preclude such activity, and the ongoing construction of news houses even complicated the formula. Something was amiss. The immediate conclusion seemed that all his animals had "abandoned ship" for this side of the river. Animals stay clear of danger – they have to stay clear, as they have no other recourse. Humans, on the other hand, have weapons that can increase their killing efficacy. Humans have stand-off weapons; guns, arrows and such. Humans also have laws designed for organizations, flow of society and behavior, as well as attorneys, police, and military. Each item listed brings a structure designed to create predictability, order, and a higher level of safety to our day-to-day lives.

The animals in Clint's familiar spot should not have located to the side of the river where man, with his loud banging, engines, radios, et al. was at, that they did, signaled a change in the local world. That change most likely meant danger and danger must be left alone, – a key animal predisposition you will see honored by the authors throughout this book.

The owner of his own tracking and survival school and the author of over a dozen books on the subject, Tom Brown Jr., is by general consensus, one of the leaders in this field, a master tracker. Clint, having studied at the Tom Brown Tracker School, was afflicted with a particular ambition, encouraged by the master tracker himself. Tom often challenged his student's abilities in stealth with the "touch the deer" test. The test was simple in the idea, yet a huge challenge, take a little hair off an unsuspecting deer. To make it a little more interesting, do it without the deer knowing that it has been actually touched by a human. Success in this test was proof that the student could stalk close enough that they couldn't miss with a primitive weapon, such as a stone or spear, in a survival situation. A week later, Clint got his chance.

Spend enough time in the outdoors and you begin to notice things that are out of place. Clint had just come out of the deer path that led down to his river sitting spot when he noticed the bushes down the path. They were moving… differently. A slight breeze was blowing one direction, but the salmonberry brush ahead seemed to be moving counter to that breeze. With the amount of brush moving, he knew it wasn't a raccoon or anything that size, and that meant a deer! He immediately went into slow motion stalk mode. It took about fifteen minutes, but by moving slowly and staying to the shadows he eventually made it to the bushes and in dappled sunlight, through the openings he saw brown fur. Triumph was near until the gigantic hiss exploded out of the brush. A tawny yellow eye looked back at him. Not a deer! Cougar! It was a high, high, stress moment.

Clint didn't turn and run, he froze. Running would have been truly foolish, as cats instinctively chase fleeing prey, instead, Clint began to walk backward quietly down the trail, apologizing profusely. The cougar, possibly out of a sense of the unusual, or a full belly, chose not to move on Clint.

There is nothing that will ratchet up your awareness like an encounter with a predator.

Clint's awareness from this point on was on much higher alert – every bush seemed a bit more sinister but nothing materialized. Weeks passed with no further incident – no cougars and few other animals crossed his path until, on a trip to his sitting spot, Clint spotted some fresh tracks. The tracks, which bisected his sitting area, were cougar tracks. The message was sent. Few of the other animals were hanging around the big cats' hunting area, and the cougar had made it clear with its tracks that while Clint might consider this his sitting area, it was, in fact, the cougar's. Message received. Maybe it was time to take a break from these woods. A few weeks exploring other environments might be a good idea.

But these woods were just down the street at a dead end that led right to the forest edge and they called to him. The wind in the cedar, the rain on the moss, all just made Clint a bit homesick for his "home" area. And always having the intention of returning to the woods Clint waited the cougar out, giving it time to move on to another end of its territory. Finally, it was time to explore the woods again, so he headed for the river spot, this time with a Kabar knife on his belt.

However, it was going to be an intense day. Clint was walking through the cedar forest on well-worn elk trails. The day was bright, and spears of sunshine shot into the ground through the boughs of the trees. Clint felt confident – being a good-sized human it was unlikely that any animal would make the effort to engage with him.

He had gone about a mile and a half when the first unusual thing happened. A common bird, a robin, appeared – a female with her duller orange underbelly, and landed on a small tree on the right side of the trail. She landed in a safe place, just the perfect height so that a human couldn't possibly reach her, and she began to alarm call. Clint, of course, thought that she was alarming the forest about him. He walked toward the robin. As he closed the distance between them, he found that he was getting unusually close – it was odd that she would let him do so. In allowing Clint to get so close, the robin sent a secondary message; the alarm was not about Clint. Instead of the low-level "tut tut" call that robins usually use with humans (robins practically live with people – if you have a yard, chances are good that it is part of a robin's territory), this robin was practically shrieking. Clint looked harder at the bird; it was not looking at Clint. The pattern was clear. The robin was safe from Clint; he had given the bird no reason to react as strongly as it was doing. As the bird continued its unusual call, it was looking past him, behind him. The hair on the back of Clint's neck began to rise and he looked behind him - nothing.

Clint, with what can be only described as hyper-vigilance, walked another 15 yards down the trail. He continued to watch his avian alarm as her red-breasted mate landed at almost the same height on a tree on the opposite side of the trail, and also began frantically calling at something behind Clint. The adrenaline pumped into his body, opening the capillaries to allow for greater blood flow to the muscles. His eyes dilated and his heartbeat increased. Clearly, the cougar was still in this territory, and was on the hunt. Clint took a breath and centered himself. He took a glance backward over his shoulder and still saw nothing.

Moving faster to gain distance from the cougar, Clint now passed a third bird, a male woodpecker, sounding another alarm. Clint thought, "OK, OK, I got it." The cat was closer. The most basic form of self-preservation, getting distance, appeared to be a poor course of action now. Clint began to look for a place to stand and fight. He needed to use the woods to, in essence, fortify his position.

The adrenal dump was now in full swing, the hard breathing, the heart pounding, It was getting difficult to manage the processing of information, the clues from the birds, seeking a spot from which to get some protection, the idea that he may have to fight a big cat. As odd as it may sound, the idea of his dead carcass, treed by the big cat and fed on for several days, was another horrifying thought that went through his mind. Panic was about three seconds away. Swiftly Clint moved 15 yards down the trail to a spot where a big hemlock tree had fallen across the trail. Someone with a chain saw had cut out the section over the trail leaving "walls" on each side of the trail from the large trunk. He dropped down between them and pulled out his Ka-Bar knife with its seven-inch blade (which suddenly seemed incredibly small). Squatting in the woods, clutching a knife, Clint could only wait, wait and listen to the signals the birds continued to give him. Suddenly there was movement! Fifty yards behind, in a salmonberry bush. Clint thought he saw a flash of tawny fur moving left to right. The birds continued to cry out.

Clint continued to hold his position in his forest fortress, or at least

as close to a fortress as he could muster. Ten minutes passed. Clint
continued to scan the bushes, no movement, no bushes rattled. The
birds stopped with their alarm calls, and after a short time, began
their normal feeding behavior. The encounter with the unknown
predator, assumed to be a cougar, had passed. Clint stood up from
between the logs, took a breath or two to clear his body, sheathed his
knife and mouthed a "thank you" to the birds.

Awareness of signals in surrounding (bird alarms in this case)
allowed Clint to realize he was being stalked.

Paying attention to the signals that are given freely by the surrounding environment can be the difference between life and death.
Ignoring such signals is done at a person's own risk. Most people, had
they even noticed the behavior of the birds, would have just ignored
it. They wouldn't have the mental training to recognize the pattern.

There are similar indicators in the modern human world. They are
broken down into patterns and behaviors. The recognition of pattern
is a normal and intrinsic part of human behavior.

Audio Pattern

Have you ever exited a sporting event where the crowd is filing out in an orderly fashion and then without warning somebody lets loose with a major yelp, or yell? Maybe a whoop of excitement over a great victory, or an expletive over a horrible loss? What happens to you? Your body? Just for a split second you tense up. You acknowledge the event and turn your attention to the noise to make a threat assessment. You also assess the others in the crowd to see how they are responding. You are treating other people the same way that Clint used the little birds in his situation with the cougar to assess the threat. In the world of the sporting event, and notably in the time after the game, you are using the other people just as Clint used the birds. Multiple resources are being used to help you decide if you have a drunk, an angry fan, or a drunken angry fan, unencumbered by social norms, that is now a threat.

Gross Physical Pattern

As the little birds flutter and jump about, so do people. There are two types of physical patterns, neither of which would you care to

The man on the right may be the alpha male in the board room, but the one on the left is alpha on the street.

participate in. The first is the attraction, this is a natural predisposition to see what is happening. This is what violence expert Rory Miller, in his book,
"Facing Violence: Preparing for the Unexpected" calls social violence and asocial violence. Social violence brings order to a moment, as it establishes a social order, it identifies the Alpha and the subordinates. Wolves have one Alpha male per pack. The Alpha Male leads the pack, mates, and keeps order. Alpha Males are challenged by subordinate Beta Males as a course of business. These Beta Males are younger than the established Alpha Male and are looking to move up. When Betas do challenge an Alpha Male the response from the Alpha is swift and violent. In these challenges, more often than not, neither the challenger nor the challenged are killed in the skirmish. That would be bad for the pack and bad for the species. Simply put, order is established. This is social violence. We are not going to go to far into the social dynamics of this type of violence because for our purposes violence is violence and needs to be avoided, just like non-predators avoid predators.

The human version of Social Violence can be identified quickly by two simple indicators, a crowd gathered and cheering. The spectacle designed to be seen, to be witnessed by all so there will be no question about who the Alpha dog is, who is in charge, who is the big dog. Asocial violence is identified by fleeing people and screaming. Think of a city-state from around 1300 AD and you hear the Mongols are on the move and heading your way. The Mongols with the reputation of city destroyers, killing those that resist, executing the captured, enslaving those of value, looting all goods, and finally burning the remnants to the ground. The Mongols built no nation, created no great written works, and left little culture, the Mongols engaged in asocial violence. You, hearing of their advancement, rightfully gather your family and flee.

Smaller Physical Pattern

Two types of body patterns can aid you in assessing a threat, just like Clint used the birds to assess the situation in which he found himself. Most non-predator humans in potential-threat situations will freeze. Truth be told everybody freezes, it is just that the freeze response for those that understand physical violence is less detectable;

for professionals, such as elite military forces, even less so. However, for most of us, the freeze looks like this; a straightened spine, and wide-open eyes. These two things are the body's way of structuring awareness; straight spine equals higher line of sight and the ability to see more / acquire more information. Further, the open eyes are another form of opening the channels and getting information.

The freeze is a simple animal reflex. The freeze is a "don't see me" move. It seems an oxymoron to say the freeze is a move, but it is a deliberate act of non-action. The brain is trying to deal with all the information, the newness of the information. If the information is old, or has been experienced before, the brain will quickly recognize, categorize and acknowledge the information for what it is – or least appears to be. The processing of new information, in the form of a potential violent encounter, can have a freeze aspect to it because it is presented quickly and threateningly. This is where seeing the adjacent pattern (for example, the birds' behavior) to the potential violence is the key to avoidance. Letting others do the work, the warning, and recognizing those warnings.

1. Listen. A group goes from being loud to quiet, or from quiet to loud.

2. Watch for group attraction (indicating social violence) or group repulsion (showing asocial violence) – both are things to avoid.

Watch other people's body language. Open eyes and straight spine are two key indicators

What constitutes a predator? Essentially, there are two classic and basic constituents; the physical and the mental. When the mind type and the body structure that is unique to the predator are combined correctly you get an animal, or a person, that is designed to dominate and exploit it's environment – to extract the resources from the world around them that they need for survival, or to meet their desires, efficiently, swiftly and mercilessly.

Stalk v. Ambush

Stalking and ambushing are two very successful methods of predatory behavior. Stalking is the act of deciding on what is a target and actively pursuing that target. Ambushing is based on the simple principle of lie and wait. A pack of wolves is an excellent example of a stalking predator and an alligator an example of an ambush predator. However, both being adaptive and being predators, the wolf can use ambush techniques when needed, and the alligator can stalk when the situation for stalking presents itself.

The wolf pack goes to where there is a known resource, whether that resource is deer, elk, or domestic cattle. The wolves begin to stalk the herd until an individual can be cut from the herd and then eventually attacked, succumbing to the wolves.

A trapdoor spider is an excellent example of an ambush predator burrowing into the ground. It builds a trapdoor on top of its burrow, hence its name, and disguises it with the local topography – sand, twigs, whatever is immediately available. Then the spider lies in wait until a potential meal gets close enough to the trapdoor. When it does, the spider leaps out, seizes the prey and in the blink of an eye pulls the victim into its burrow for consumption.

Animals kill and eat their prey; that is the resource that they are after. This is not news. The prey is a resource, a necessary aspect of the predator's survival. As humans, we have differing perspectives on the morality of considering the animals in our world to be merely resources, a necessary aspect of our survival. Often, a person that chooses to be a vegetarian does so out of a sense of the wrongness of this perspective. They feel that we as humans have a choice, and we should choose not to kill other animals for our survival. Humans can survive without killing other animals, as we are omnivores. Animals such as the cheetah, panther, lion, and tiger, have literally no option but to kill to survive. Their nutritional needs are met almost entirely from the flesh of other animals.

Humans on the other hand don't kill each other to consume one another; cannibalism is taboo for the majority of the world and only engaged in under extreme circumstances. An example would be the famous true story recounted in the film *Alive: The Story of the Andes Survivors* (1974). It is an account of the surviving members of a soccer

We are predators, it's how we survived for untold millennia.
It's when we prey on each other that the dark side dominates.

team whose airplane crashed in the Andes Mountains and their need to resort to cannibalism to survive. No person, to the authors' knowledge, has ever condemned these men for engaging in cannibalism for their survival. It isn't about the content of what happened, it is about the context in which it happened.

So outside of extraordinarily disturbed people like Albert Fish, an American serial killer and cannibal, or Ed Gein, the inspiration for the Texas Chainsaw Massacre movie, almost all predatory behavior of humans and non-humans alike is about resources; "You have something; I want it."

Tangible and Intangible Resources

Animals are all about the tangible resource, being able to eat the flesh of another animal. Humans, as we've pointed out, don't often engage in the consumption of each other, yet they still engage in predatory behavior.

This means that the tangible resource is different. The resource that the victim/target has is something that the predator desires, or possibly needs for survival. Money (including credit cards, checks or ATM cards) is the most obvious choice of a resource. A secondary resource would be something that can be converted into money such as a watch or mobile phone. Thirdly, there are the resources that can be used to meet a need, such as a car to move from one location to another. Resources can be thought of as tangible and intangible. Tangible resources are broken into two categories immediately useful and transferable.

Intangible resources can be broken down into two categories: external and internal. An example of an external intangible resource is that of status – status within your peer group, especially if you are a gang member or you have a clique with which the predator associates. It is important to have status within that gang or clique. One way to establish credibility and status on the organizational ladder within the group is to perpetrate a crime on a victim that can be documented. It can then be seen or validated by the peer members of the associated gang or clique. The act may be reported in the local media, or recorded on a cell phone, to provide proof to the group of the predator's act.

Internal intangibles are associated with bully behavior. There is an internal need for validation resulting from the predator's, or bully's, lack of emotional resources. We don't want to go into the dynamics of how bullies are created; we are concerned with the interaction between the bully and the victim in regard to meeting their resource needs.

Internal Intangible Resources

There is a hole in the emotional makeup of bullies, and they attempt to fill that hole with their actions. Their bully behavior is designed to satisfy that emotional hole. The type of behavior bullies can engage in may border on sadism; one could go so far so far as to call it a form of torture. Internal intangible needs are often difficult to understand, and are never fulfilled only forestalled.

Specialization of Environment

Animals specialize by environment. They are segregated into land, air and water. Humans, on the other hand, are almost exclusively involved in predation on land. Only a small percentage of humans actually fish for existence, or hunt birds, yet in the modern world we can all partake of these resources because of role exclusivity. We have fishermen and hunters that share their kill. The only time that humans exhibit predator behavior in a large scale on water, or air, against other humans are during acts of war. War is an act of resource.

Human predators specialize in a path of success for predatory behavior. That is to say they learn predatory behavior from others. They then find success with the adopted behavior and continue to repeat it. In the animal kingdom, predators use the same method of determining, and then using, "go to" methods of predation.

Think of it this way; it would seem almost comical to imagine an alligator charging over long distances of ground, like a wolf, in pursuit of its prey. Ridiculous, ridiculous for a number of reasons. The alligator doesn't have a bone or muscle structure designed to cover long distances of ground swiftly, its cardiovascular system and respiratory system are ill-suited to long-distance predatory behavior such as what a mammal can accomplish, it simply is a comical picture. That's not to say that alligators don't demonstrate instances of straight, short-burst running over ground. But for our purposes we can see how unrealistic such a thing appears.

Specialization of the predator takes place externally and internally. Externally, the environment determines how successful the predator will be. For example, the alligator is very successful in the swamp, and the wolf is successful in flat, open spaces. Now we can argue whether or not nature placed the predator into the environment or the predator adapted to the environment, but we are not really interested in that argument. What we are interested in is the matching of the external environment and the internal predator. Many movies are based on this misplacement of the predator. The classic movie Crocodile Dundee (Paramount Pictures 1986) is a misplaced predator, albeit an affable one, who after wrestling with alligators and battling predators from all

domains in his native Australia winds up in the "urban jungle" of New York City. Here he is misunderstood, and underestimated by people from all walks of life, including the urban predator who brandishes the knife demanding Crocodile Dundee's money, resulting in the now-iconic phrase, "Now that's a knife," uttered by Crocodile Dundee as he brandishes his Bowie knife in front of the urban predator. This of course is fiction, enjoyable fun, but fiction nonetheless.

Chapter Two
How Nature Builds a Predator

"Efficiency is doing things right; effectiveness is doing the right things."
–Peter Drucker

As we discussed with the wolf and the alligator, these two animals are well suited enough for their environments to be, if not at the top of the food chain, very close. If these two animals transposed envi-

The alligator uses his environment to attack by surprise. How do human predators do this?

ronments, wolf to the swamp, and alligator to the woods, they would be dead within a short time. Further if, these animals knew how to escape that transposed environment and return to their known environment they would do it as fast as possible because they intuitively understand that they are ill-suited for the environment in which they have been placed.

Nature builds specific predators, whether it's for land, water, or sky. Nature goes so far as to create predators for the subtypes of each environment. In the land subtypes of desert, forest, and plains, specific skills and tools are required. As the land has different environments the sky has different altitudes. Little birds, such as chickadees and robins, stay closer to the ground; larger birds, predator birds, stay high in the air. Hawks and eagles want to survey the land for their next potential meal. The sea world is divided by freshwater and saltwater, and within that there are strata. As we all know, not all fish are the same. A fish placed in water that has the incorrect saline level for its species will soon die. Fish are also pressure sensitive. Some fish stay very close to the surface of the water while others very deep and some are able to move through multiple levels. Nature's work is broad and deep, yet it is also specific, and very exacting. Nature builds the predator for the environment. On the other hand, people who choose to become predators, although there are exceptions, build themselves for their environment.

As we've already discussed, the alligator is an excellent example of a predator built for its environment. It is cold blooded and lives in warm climates; being cold-blooded means that the alligator has a slower metabolism, it doesn't generate its own heat and has a slower digestive rate and a lower daily calorie intake. Alligators are camouflaged they can appear to be a log to an unsuspecting victim and can sit motionless for hours. They can also be submerged for extended periods of time. Their jaws are very strong and when snapping shut can exert approximately 3,500 pounds per square inch as they clamp down on their prey. But the human hand can hold the alligator mouth closed because the muscles are so weak in regard to opening their jaw. This disparity of muscle distribution is demonstrated by alligator wranglers and sideshow men on a daily basis. The alligator is capable of very explosive straight-line forward movement, but has very little lateral movement. Their predatory behavior is simple; wait for prey to come into the proximity of their strike zone and then strike in an explosive thrust forward. Alligators can also approach the prey stealthily and lock them in their jaws. Regardless of the approach and strike, the alligator then pulls the prey under the water and begins the death roll, where the alligator spins the prey's body over and over again, tearing chunks of flesh each time and killing it. Once the prey is dead it is consumed in a large gulp of flesh with no regard to whether the alligator is consuming fin or feather.

The human predator is similar in many ways to both the alligator and the wolves. However, the human is more flexible. While it lacks the natural weapons with which those in the animal kingdom are born, we can stand upright. This ability gives a constant and natural overview of our immediate area. Humans also can climb on rocks or

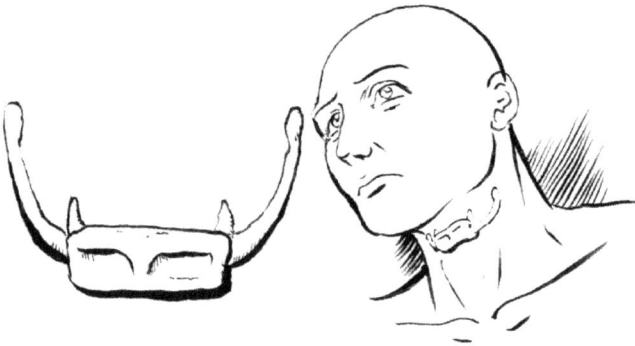

Hyoid bone.

up trees, swim to escape or seek food, and run. The three key physical attributes that separate us from the animal kingdom are the cerebral cortex, the Hyoid bone, and the bones in the hand that allow for precise movement of the fingers, and most importantly, the thumb.

The human predator can hunt solo like an alligator or in packs like wolves. Yet

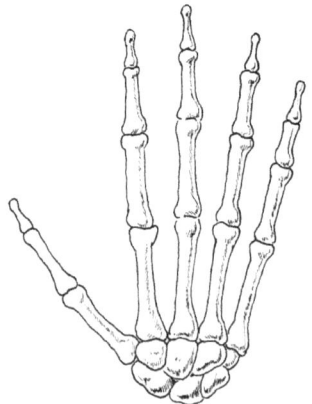

Bones of the human hand.

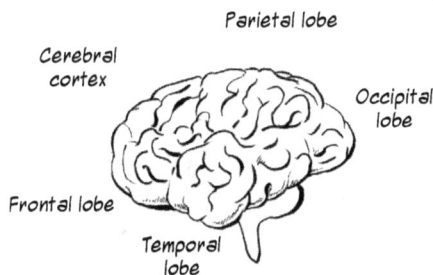

Parietal lobe

Cerebral cortex

Occipital lobe

Frontal lobe

Temporal lobe

human predators develop preferred methods that are best suited to their environment. They use these methods over and over again because, just like the animal world, there is no need to tamper with success.

Solo v. Pack Mentality

A solo human predator can be divided into two types, the Solo Competent Predator and the Solo Insane Predator. Each can be equally dangerous.

Solo Competent Predator

The Solo Competent Predator is a very effective predator. If there is safety in numbers, there is confidence in a solo act of predation. The Solo Competent Predators, develop their skill, and the competence attached to that skill, from the fact that they have done what they have done multiple times, even hundreds of times, and have been very successful. In other words, with regard to their predatory activities, the metaphorical training wheels are off. They are now able to work solo effectively. This confidence in the Solo Competent Predator also indicates that, through their methods and the sheer volume of the times they have perpetuated this crime, you as the prey have little recourse -- this is your first time while this is their one-hundredth. These predators know what they want and how to get it in an efficient manner. You are a resource to them, or possibly an impediment to them getting the resource they want. There's no negotiation, there is no hoodwinking the Solo Competent Predator. If they are threatened or they sense things are going bad, they will use violence to ensure their desired results.

Solo Insane Predator

Rabies is a viral brain disease that is transmitted by bites, from animal to animal and sometimes to humans. The virus attacks the brain, making the animal violent and unpredictable. Rabies is fatal. Rabies causes unstable, violent, and irrational behavior. In the same vein, drug usage causes unstable, violent and irrational behavior. Mental illness, when not treated, can manifest in the same way. We would never think to try to get a late-term, rabies-infected dog to obey a command of "Sit" or "Come". The outward manifestation of these con- ditions would make all rational people get distance and stay clear. The Solo Insane Predator, similarly, can broadcast itself, and any attempt to rationalize with them is tantamount to attempting to rationalize with the rabies-infected dog. Their brains are mush, and only the most basic functions originating from the lower brain functions are in place. These Solo Insane Predators may well be drug-addled, experiencing some form of withdrawal, or even hunger. Regardless, these individuals are not in their right mind. Contrast this with the Competent Solo Predator, who if you of- fer no resistance to the resource you are likely to walk away with no injuries, The Solo Insane Predator, on the other hand, could respond in a variety of unpredictable ways – lurching with a weapon, perceiving you to be a demon and in need of killing, or at- tacking you purely because your movement was seen as a threat.

Humans Kill More Humans

Animals will kill those of their own species; a lion when taking over a pride will kill the cubs of the former lion that led the pride. Ani- mals will also eat their own species, such as eating their own young in large quantities as some fish do. And there are the occasions of animals turning on their own species when there is food scarcity.

However no animal kills for as many varied reasons as humans. Humans will kill like lions do, for example, with regard to youth that are in line for leadership positions or kingdoms. Richard the III the

King of England during the late 1400s was believed to have ordered the removal, the killing, of two princes that could be considered rivals. History is rife with examples of fratricide. Competing with the existing leader is a formula for banishment or extermination. There are also instances of humans eating other humans; for example, the stories of Christian crusaders, from the book, *Crusades Through Arab Eyes* by Amin Maalouf. The author quotes Radulph of Caen, an eye-witness to what occurred at Ma'arra in 1098, "In Ma'arra our troops boiled pagan adults in cooking-pots; they impaled children on spits and devoured them grilled." There is also mass killing by political leaders. Joseph Stalin (1878–1953) oversaw the death of some 4 to 10 million people, depending on the record, personally signing off on the deaths of his own people, prisoners of war, and undesirables via execution, forced internment, or forced relocation.

10 Million

5 Million

1 Million

Those in charge of governments occasionally evolve into genocidal super predators.

What separates humans from animals in regard to killing is the large brain of the human and the use of diverse and creative tools. The large cerebral cortex leads and the creative tools follow. A person doesn't need to go very far to list the types of weapons that have been created to kill other human beings, of course. We almost have to start with the rock and the stick, but soon the rock becomes attached to the stick and becomes a stone mace; and soon a leather strap attached to the back of the spear allows the spear to be thrown farther and harder than the opponent.

Arrows are replaced by bolts, crossbows begin to pierce armor, siege machines, fire, flooding, biological warfare, starvation, garrotes, decapitation, evisceration, scourging, crucifixion, poison, swords, knives, cannonballs, exploding cannonballs, artillery rounds, aircraft, ships, submarines, and the list goes on ad nauseam culminating with the atomic bomb.

The reason for all of these creative ways of exterminating another human being, again, is all about, "You have something and I want that," or "You don't believe what I believe."

Animals are environment-specific; humans are able to take the environment they need for survival with them. In fact the human race is represented on all of the seven continents of the earth. Clearly the brain and the creativity that comes from brain size are contributing factors to the widespread presence of the human predator.

Nature adapts predators to their environment, and then subdivides and stratifies the animal even further, creating specialization. Humans have penetrated almost every environment. Outside of a few very extreme environments such as the deepest sea and highest mountain, man has spread across the globe.

The predatory animals that make their homes in these environments bring with them no such thing as morals and judgments when it comes to killing. They kill with the tools they were born with; tooth, fang, claw or poison. Humans have created innumerable ways of killing members of the animal kingdom and their own human race, always for extracting the resource or ending a threat real or imagined.

Chapter Three

Nature Adapts Predators to Their Environment

"Adapt or perish, now as ever, is nature's inexorable imperative."

- H.G. Wells

Whether it's the wolf or the alligator that we have used so far, it's clear that predators are built for their environment and make adaptions to their environment to be successful.

In using the comparison between these two animals we are attempting to make a stark contrast between the acute skills and adaptations that each has made for their specific environments. The wolf is a mammal, controlling its own body heat and covered in fur; the alligator is a reptile subject to the ambient temperature of its environment and covered in scales. These two predators dominate in their environments and yet their structures could not be more different.

Wolf

When it comes to the offensive structure of the wolf, the adaption list is large. The wolf possesses a nose with a keen sense of smell; it is always moistened, it is able to capture and process smells with great efficiency and discernment. The canine teeth used for tearing the flesh are large and sharp; the jaw strong for capturing, holding down, killing and eventually consuming its prey. The wolf has a thick chest and powerful shoulder muscles to assist the long legs in fast pursuit. The wolf possesses large paws, displacing its weight over a larger surface area and allowing it to deftly cover varied terrain. The wolf has four toes on its hind legs and five toes on its fore feet, providing an extra claw on each foot. This extra claw assists in traction when shifting positions while in pursuit as well as being clearly useful when attacking prey. The wolf has large ears with acute hearing and is able to move their ears in the direction needed to hear the movements of

Eyes - set in front of skull
for stereoscopic vision.
(Depth perception)

Nose - elongated snout
for better sense of smell

Legs - long and
lean for running up
to 20 miles a day.

Jaws - very strong, designed for
crushing and ripping

Paws/claws - designed
for traction in the
sprint, not as weapons.

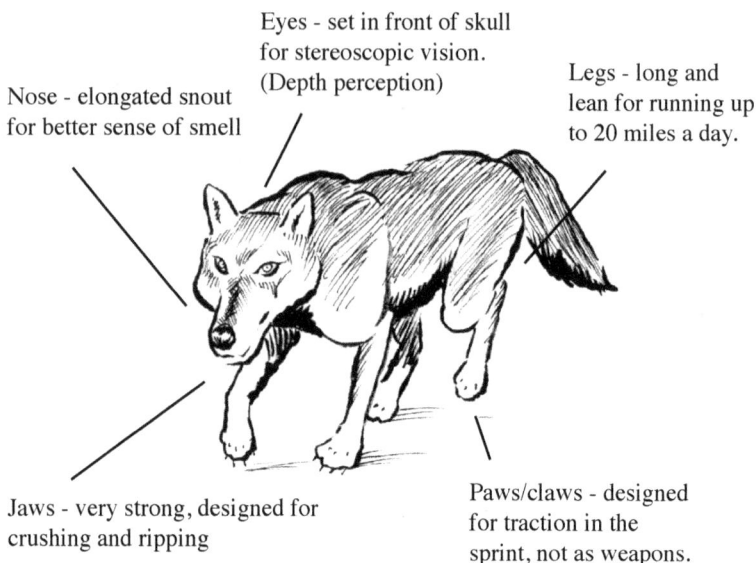

Designing a predator.
(Canis lupus)

its prey. Wolves are also equipped with excellent eyesight. Further, the wolf walks on its toes; and in particular, when looking at the back leg you can see that the heel of the wolf's hind legs are actually about a third of the way up its legs. A simple rule of nature is "the higher the heel the faster the animal." In total, nature has created a profoundly efficient predator. As nature is not inclined to waste much, the wolf's weapons for hunting also serve as its means of defense, with the notable exception of its thick mane. Around the neck, it assists in the protection of one of the most vulnerable parts of its body. This thick coat of fur also extends across the entire body; again protecting the wolf from some forms of injury and serving as protection from the elements.

Alligator

The alligator is a very linear and forward-oriented animal. That is to say that it is long and the business end of the alligator is all up front. The head of the alligator can constitute up to an entire fifth of its body, its mouth containing up to 80 teeth in all. All 80 of the teeth are designed for snatching and holding its prey. There are no molars in the alligator's mouth for grinding. The eyes as well as the nostrils of the alligator are placed on top of the head. This eye and nostril placement allows the alligator to be partially submerged and yet view its surroundings and breathe easily. On dry land, while the alligator can be fast in short bursts, it has no sustained speed because it walks on its heels as opposed to the wolf with its high heel placement.

Further, the legs of the alligator are splayed out, arcing out and away from the body. This makes it difficult for the alligator to carry its body load on land yet it makes for a very adroit swimmer, as the alligator is able to move all four legs in a sophisticated and independent manner. The webbing between the toes gives the alligator extra purchase in the water, allowing it to move swiftly as the webs capture a larger surface area of the water. The tail of an alligator is another notable feature. Taking up one third of its body mass, it is composed of powerful muscles and can be used in the same way that the fish would use its tail for propulsion. But, because it is a tail and not a fin, it can be used to create the alligator death roll. Simply put, the alligator seizes its prey in its jaws, submerges the prey, and then begins to spin using its long tail to create the spinning action. This death roll technique would be impossible if the alligator possessed a fin in lieu of a tail. The alligator is also covered with hard body plates, the hardest being on its back and sporting what could best be called small horns. These hard plates serve as an ever-present and passive form of defense.

Humans

Humans are often called "The naked ape." The reason for this term is that humans possess no claws like the wolf, or the protective scales of the alligator that protect their bodies. Also, the human heels are low, which allow for the carrying of large loads over distance, but not for generating much speed when trying to escape a predator or chase a possible meal as a wolf would do.

The human has some advantages in regard to survival and predatory behavior, however the first and largest advantage that humans have is the cerebral cortex. The cerebral cortex covers the outer part of the cerebrum in a thick cap. It allows for creative thought and the ability to contemplate actions and the results of those actions.

The importance of the human brain in regard to humans' predatory behavior cannot be understated. It is the author's opinion that the modern human or Cro-Magnon man, with the brain of say a wolf, or an alligator would be extinct as a species very quickly, consumed by other predators so fast as to quite possibly never have a chance to propagate. The ability to fashion weapons, to premeditate killing, to build traps, and out-think its prey is what sets the

The brain makes this naked ape the most successful predator on the planet

human apart from the animal kingdom. The cerebral cortex is what makes humans human. The cerebral cortex sits upon the mammalian brain sometimes called the midbrain, which is composed of sections like the amygdala and the thalamus and governs basic body behaviors, such as emotions like fear. The lizard brain, or old brain serves the basic bodily functions. Many books have been written on brain performance, brain types, and the interplay of these three brains. We will not go into much detail about this because others have done it better and in more detail. Further the volume of the work is enormous. Suffice it to say that this one organ, a mere three pounds in weight, has been the nexus for travel in outer space, exploration, selfless love, and the extermination of millions of its own kind.

The hyoid bone and the larynx are not unique to humans. In fact they can be found in many species of animals, but how they are used by humans is unique. What the hyoid bone does is aid in tongue movement. Located in front of the human throat between the chin and the top of the Thyroid, the hyoid bone does not rest against other bones; it sits suspended in space anchored by muscles. This bone allows for a higher level of tongue articulation and a lowered larynx in the human throat, which combine to serve as a mechanism for the most sophisticated means of communication the planet has ever known, the spoken language. Language is so successful that it patterns nature. Nature has many ways to solve problems but cannot compare to the problem-solving power of language. Not only does language allow for numerous ways to solve a problem, the world has close to 7000 languages in which to discuss and solve problems.

The opposeable thumb. The opposeable thumb is not unique to humans either – apes, monkeys and chimpanzees, to name a few, possess opposeable thumbs. Yet there is a difference between the human hand and the ape hand. These differences in bones are slight but significant. One bone in particular, the trapezium bone on which the thumb bones (metacarpal and phalanges) rest upon, serves as a single pivot point that separates the sophisticated human hand from the ape's, allowing for greater range of motion and more sophisticated usage.

The combination of these three things, a few more ounces of gray matter, a bone placed a little lower in the throat, and a small bone in the hand the size of a pebble give us the ability to solve complex problems, discuss displaced phenomena and execute precise and exacting hand movements. The ability of language and the ability for polished hand movements give the human predator the upper hand when it comes to survival, predation, and ultimately world dominance as a species.

Chapter Four
Peacocks and Wolf Tails

"The supreme art of war is to subdue the enemy without fighting."
– Sun Tzu

Peacocks are vibrant birds. Peacocks' plumes are made of vibrant blues and greens. The Peacock also has the ability to spread its enormous tail feathers, forming a wall of colorful blues, golds, greens, browns, and whites and taking up space some three times its body size. These displays are designed to attract the peahen for mating purposes. The display also carries with it colored dots. These dots resemble eyes and serve at the same time as a bluff and warning to territorial invaders, or potential male competitors.

Wolves run in packs, an extended family numbering around 4-7 members, sometimes more. The social structure is simple and strictly enforced. The pack is run by the Alpha Male and the Alpha Female. These two alone are allowed to breed, and they are the only members that are allowed to hold their tails high, all other tails in the pack must be down. Wolves also display dominance by standing on their hind legs to gain height. Subservient wolves roll on their backs exposing their vulnerable bellies. Now there are more subtleties of dominant and submissive behavior as well as other forms of tail placement used to communicate emotions and status within the pack, but we won't go into them here.

Humans are part peacock and part wolf

Peacocking is a slang term used to indicate that somebody is preening and displaying clothing and possessions to demonstrate virility and earning power. This peacocking behavior is over-the-top behavior used to separate the "peacock" from the rest of the group. Human predators will also peacock to people outside of their group, as well as use other forms of display to establish dominance. However when hunting, stealth is the key.

Tattoos

Tattoos have become a very popular form of declaring individuality. Placement of the tattoo is as significant as the design. A dolphin or unicorn on a middle-aged woman is very different from a full-colored sleeve on the arm of a constructor worker. These two forms of tattoos are similar in that they are peacock behavior. A third form, the prison tattoo, is not. Instead, it is typically either a declaration of a gang affiliation or a symbol of death and/or killing.

Hair

The Goths, before the term was co-opted to refer to a malcontent teenager with a makeup box, were a Germanic tribe. The Goths played a key role in the downfall of the Roman Empire. They would grow their hair long, and often dye it and mound it on top of their heads, increasing their already towering height over the Roman legionaries. Hair can be used to peacock, as well as the lack of hair. In the case of a man, a deliberate bald head can be the public equivalent to having his shirt off, a clear dominance display.

Sunglasses

The old saying, "The eyes are the window to the soul" is true. That is why police detectives have made a study of eye placement and the corresponding level of truth of the person being interrogated. Sunglasses hide the eyes, obfuscating the "tells" that the eyes might give. When you cannot see the eyes it makes it more difficult to see and sense intent and emotion.

Attitude of a Predator

In the animal world the attitude of a predator is fairly straightforward. For the most part, it consists of "Am I hungry?", "Is that other animal food?", and "How much trouble/risk will it be to make a kill?"

Predators in the wild want their kill as easy as possible. They can't afford to get injured badly, because an injured hunter can't hunt. If they can't hunt, they and their offspring won't live to pass on their genes. However if they want their prey, they have no qualms about killing, they just do what's needed.

Human predators have a much greater variety of reasons to hunt their own kind (and make no mistake, for most, crime is their form of hunting). Sometimes it's simply transferring resources from a victim, but other times it's a need to transfer power. Robbers, burglars and thieves generally want the main human "meat" that we all seek, money (and yes, this is a very broad generalization). Rapists and serial killers hunt for power over, and the degradation/death of, their prey. Dominance is the meat they seek.

The main thing you can count on that all of the above two-legged predators have in common is that: they have no consideration for you as a human being. You are simply a source of fulfillment of their needs.

It is sometimes hard for normal people to understand this other than in the most general Hollywood movie terms. Most people would feel bad if a person fell down a staircase and injured themselves, so it's hard to believe that there are others who are capable of pushing someone down those stairs. It is very hard to wrap your head around evil if you're not evil yourself. But make no mistake, you are nothing to these people. Your only connection to them is as a potential victim of violence of one sort or another.

This is why it is better to learn to identify the predators early, before they're in striking distance so that you can mount a defense or escape and evade.

Solo and Group Predators

There are two types of hunting and two types of criminal activity. When you compare them across the animal kingdom with human behavior you find some very clear similarities.

Solo animal predators break down into two kinds; physically large solo predators and hyper aggressive solo predators.

Solo animal predators' behavior can be demonstrated by looking at many of the big cats. Leopards, for example, hunt by themselves, not being a pack animal to begin with and live a solo lifestyle. Anybody that has had a cat in their life can be quite aware of how, even in a group of cats, a cat is still a solitary animal. This psychology of solitude makes them solo hunters – it simply is their nature.

Group animal predators can also be exemplified by wolves or coyotes. Working in an organized pack with a social structure and an order of responsibility and implementing group behaviors that bring forth known results are the earmarks of group hunting.

Some readers may point out that coyotes will hunt on their own and kill a groundhog, a rabbit, or a mouse if the opportunity avails itself. That is because the predatory nature of the coyote supersedes the group mentality. If the animal is smaller than the predator, in this case a coyote, and the opportunity presents itself the predator simply acts.

It's interesting to note that among groups of solo predator-type animals, there are group behaviors, or the appearance of such, but they are not coordinated. An example would be a shark feeding frenzy. On the surface it may be appear the sharks are feeding together; therefore, they are cooperating. However, that is not true; they simply have massed themselves on the available food source and are feeding simultaneously. Instead of a coordinated effort, it is every shark for itself. Often, one shark will bite another in this frenzy. This form of faux group hunting is similar to violent crowd action.

Humans will hunt solo, or in groups, whatever best suits their needs. Humans employ these strategies, choosing between these two forms of predation based on a reasonable assurance of success.

Human solo predators have difficulty in forming long-lasting deep relationships. If placed in a psychological test, it is the authors' belief that these human solo predators would probably score very low on certain attributes, such as building long-lasting and meaningful relationships. The reason for this is because they see the world as a resource; they see themselves as the "top dog" and therefore have no real need for deep meaningful relationships. As for their surface needs, their resources are met.

Think of the solo human predator in the same way you would any large predator. They dominate the group in which they are a member; they use displays to demonstrate their prowess. A wolf that is the Alpha Male will hold its tail high. The human predator may well wear all black, particularly leather, as it is an animal skin, sunglasses, obfuscating their eyes, and may go with a clean-shaven head. They may also decide to combine similar attributes with a splash of peacocking. One only needs to look at a member of the Mafia, well dressed and possibly wearing some adornments in gold, a precious metal and standard exchange for humans since time immemorial. The total effect signifies wealth, success and dominance.

When the solo human predator is standing in front of you and demanding a resource from you, you're already behind the curve. The human hunter has already 1) identified you as a victim, 2) made sure that you are in a physical space where you are unable to escape/defend yourself very well, and 3) They have closed on you with speed, surprise, and violence of action – not a new formula for man or animal.

Group animal predators use the same methodologies as the solo hunter; however, such predators are often physically smaller. A group hunt may indicate younger predators, or possibly those that are not as experienced in the act of violence and predation. The simple axiom of "strength in numbers" applies here. Coyotes use strength in numbers to circle their intended meal and attack from multiple angles and multiple times. Coyotes always keep the victims off balance and unable to defend themselves. This off balancing results in the victim making a mistake and eventually succumbing to the repetitive and mass nature of the attacks. Of course, a group also has to share the rewards taken or it begins to lose members.

When looking at solo or group attacks we again can see how they are successfully, and similarly, employed in both the animal and the human world. Solo predators are confident; they are aggressive, they understand violence and are willing to use it to get whatever resource they have decided they need, they are able to act swiftly, without building consensus, and doing so with a sense of impunity.

Group predators work together; they have an established method-ology, protocols, and a pecking order governing what they do and what techniques they employ. These techniques are ingrained into the members of the group. These methods are taught to them in the predators' youth and these techniques are then tested in the field sharpening their skills.

Aggressive Cues
Context and Content

Where an aggressive behavior takes place makes all the differ-ence. If you run across a room at full speed and slam your body into another person, for instance a man, and slam him to the ground you are on the fast track to a beating from his friends and or a ride to jail. On the other hand, if you do the same thing on the rugby field you are cheered for a great tackle.

If a cougar runs down a fawn, kills it and retires to a tree or a hide with the carcass, it is nature in action. If we witness the event we might feel sad for the fawn, but recognize that it is part of the natural order of life. If the scenario remains the same, except for one differ-ence, the fawn becomes your family dog, well, the cougar just became – out of control? Dangerous? The mind races. "If that cougar will kill a dog, what is next? Our children?" The cat is deemed a threat and destroyed.

So, content is important, but context can determine everything.

Cold reading is a method used by many carneys, entertainers, and other such ilk to make estimated guesses about people, their behaviors, and personal lives, and use those clues to see the unseen. We are now going to ask you to learn how to engage in a little cold reading, an assessment exercise if you will. We will then ask you to move the results of your work to your active mind. We want you to think about, and actively assess, a person – just like an animal would, threat or no threat.

Clothing

Designer labels indicate wealth, exclusivity, and access to resources. Loud colors declare, "look at me," "see me," "take notice of me." Lack of clothing, however, is different between women and men. Scantily clothed women demonstrate availability. There are several subtexts to this form of clothing, such as demonstrating availability while seeking to cause a dust up between males. A shirtless male is a sign of aggression. However, context in both of these situations is paramount to the interpretation of the dress behavior. Shirts are no longer just for covering a person's torso; they make statements. An Affliction shirt, with its wild art based in medieval inspiration, is a dead give away to what skills the wearer thinks that they possess. When actor Leonardo DeCaprio is wearing a Hello Kitty shirt, we respond to it much differently than if Mixed Martial Arts Champion and legend Randy Couture is wearing the same shirt. Is the shirt too big for the person? The question, then, is "What are they hiding?" A tight-fitting shirt is also a statement, one of confidence in one's physical appearance.

Everyone is sending signals, some louder than others.

These questions also apply to pants. White pants worn by an office worker connote a much different vibe than a pair of dirty jeans on a biker. Further, that biker is not inclined to wear a pair of surfing shorts.

Footwear also tells you if the wearer is sporty – trainers, or sport shoes, are often worn for comfort, not training. Steel-toed boots on a construction site are the norm; the same boots in a roadhouse bar may signal an offensive intent instead of the "safety first," necessity on a work site. Flip-flops on a Samoan, of which there are many in the Seattle area, is a cultural thing. Those same flip-flops, don't allow for ease in running, as an athletic shoe would.

Ask any security officer, or police officer and they will tell you that inappropriate dress is a clue to potential action, and it draws their attention. A leather coat on a warm summer day is contextually incorrect and forces the questions, "why?" and "what are they hiding?"

A display of keys is a public pronouncement of responsibility, and with responsibility comes the

It's a hot day, why the long coat?

natural extension of power. Look at the young men that have their keys clipped to the belt loop of their pants, or the extra long lanyard hanging from their pocket – the fact is that it serves as a faux penis, and the longer the better.

Physical Body
Standing

Standing with feet wide is not normal. The human body does not what to work very hard. Like any predator in the wild, the conservation of energy is important and always respected. A fully fed lion that does not face a threat is docile. Humans who stand with their feet wider than their shoulders are using more energy than if they were to place their feet underneath their shoulders, an energy efficient way of carrying their weight. To continue with the penis theme, standing with feet wider than the shoulders is a territorial display, and a penis display. This is not a solely male action; at times aggressive females will also engage in this behavior.

Sitting

A version of the genital display is also done while sitting. Knees splayed, exposing the genitals is the same as the standing version. It can be intensified by sprawling the arms as well. This demonstrates

a casual and in-control dominance. Wilder's judo sensei would tell students that sat in Seiza (the classic Japanese sitting posture, legs folded underneath and seated on the heels) that sitting with their knees too wide was like telling everybody that you had a big one. It always garnered a laugh.

Posture

A stiff back means alertness, or wariness. Ask any animal owner and they will tell you what this means. You do not need to think too hard on this one.

Hair

Think of hair as a mane, a lion's mane if you like. The more this hair is doted on the more social value on presence the person places. The deliberate lack of hair, shaving one's head, is a sign of aggression. Now clearly some men shave their head to deal with male pattern baldness. But if that is not present, then the clean head look becomes something else – a sign of dominance.

Tattoos

There are three kinds of tattoos. There are many reasons for getting a tattoo. We will break them into three types to serve our purposes.

Pretty Boy. These tattoos are meant to be displayed; they are often on the arms, and called sleeves. They are generally expensive, they are multicolored and very well done as they are done with modern machine, a tattoo gun. They are not a warning, they may speak to the idea of the self that the owner has regarding their perceived position in life, but are not necessarily anything other than an adornment.

Prison Ink. Prison ink are monochromatic, as they are made from pen ink, blue or black, and are done in a traditional manner, without a modern tattoo gun. However that does not exclude the use of tattoo guns ingeniously built inside the jail / prison. These tattoos can serve a purpose such as gang affiliation, or as a declaration of a religious affiliation. What is said by the ink is frequently secondary to the act of the inking itself.

Cultural. You need only look to the Polynesian cultures to see the use of tattoo as symbolism that denotes rank and status within a community.

Tattoos on necks and faces make a profound statement. For example, the tear drop tattoo. However, it has many meanings, causing some confusion. It can mean that the wearer has been incarcerated, that the wearer has killed somebody, that a friend has been killed, or that a friend's death has been avenged.

Surrounding Area

Swear words. Swear words are designed to shock or to threaten. They can equate to a gorilla pulling grass and throwing it into the air. A typical warning may sound like, "Yo, bro, you want some? I'll f*#k you up, man; you're a f#@king dead man." In other words, like a monkey throwing things.

Voice volume. The louder the voice, the more escalation of aggression. Shouting over somebody is a way of winning, by being louder and more threatening that the other. Tone and volume can be great indicators as to what is happening. The squeal of a rabbit when the jaws of a coyote pinch down on it is far different from a wolf's howl, yet both are a warning.

Music. Apes don't make music, but they do beat on their environment with sticks. The intent is to establish territory. "Look at me! Whack! Look at me! Whack, Whack." Music can be the same for the same reasons. Music is and can be a time stamp. People of different ages have different tastes, an older demographic is more likely to listen to classic rock than say the latest rap artist.

Car

The larger the car, the darker the car, the higher off the ground the car, the more threat it is intended to pose. All you need do is compare any Honda Civic, regardless of how stylish the lines, and a Ford Expedition and you have your answer. Now to make up for the size, you can get your Civic painted black, maybe another power color for the hood, such as red, add a spoiler, and now you have a warning system similar to the poison-laden coral snake! Cars are about size and color; bigger is more powerful and bigger and loudly colored is the top of the food chain. You need only look at Monster Trucks, such as the lime green and purple colored "Grave Digger," for an example. By extension, if I drive such a powerful vehicle, then I must be powerful.

Sunglasses

Sunglasses are about denying others one of the most vital aspects of human communication. Wearing sunglasses for any other reason than keeping the brightness of the day out of your eyes is an act, not necessarily of aggression, but denial of intimacy.

All these clues can be used to assess the viability of solo and group predators. By taking in all of the animal clues that the subject of your observation has given, you can begin to decide a reasonable course of action that will keep you safe.

Chapter Five
Time, Distance, Exposure

"Constant exposure to dangers will breed contempt for them."
-Lucius Annaeus Seneca

In May 1996, Phil Anderson from Port Angeles, Washington planned to spend part of his day mountain biking in a National Park. Port Angeles is located in the Pacific Northwest, in Washington state, and in the furthest northwest corner of the state. It is only a slight exaggeration to say that the next U.S. port of call is Anchorage, Alaska. The trail that Anderson chose that day was the Wolf Creek trail, which runs along the Elwha River to Hurricane Ridge. The Elwha River is approximately 45 miles long, and sports some five different species of salmon as well as and other fish such as bass and trout. We suggest taking a moment and going to the National Parks of Washington website and look at the Hurricane Ridge Webcam located at: http://www.nps.gov/olym/photosmultimedia/hurricane-ridge-webcam.htm, to get a true sense of the size and density of the forest environment of the Olympic National Forest.

The path that Anderson chose that day for his mountain biking excursion was not on the edge of the wilderness, it *was* the wilderness. Before setting out, Anderson took off his large black sweatshirt, anticipating an athletic ride. The density and dampness of the Pacific Northwest forest can chill a person quickly even on the warmest days, so having a sweatshirt handy is a good idea. If you're not active, the cold can set in quite quickly. In what would turn out to be a two-hour ride, he decided to leave his sweatshirt at the trailhead.

After an invigorating ride, he returned to the trailhead where he had begun his ride. After dismounting from his bike and removing his helmet it was now time to protect himself from the coolness of the forest. Anderson popped his head through the neck hole of his sweatshirt. With his heavy sweatshirt secured over his chest Anderson caught the smooth motion of a soon-to-be combatant out of the corner of his eye. "He just moved out of the shadows, so smoothly and quickly." The young cougar, that Anderson later estimated to be about 80 pounds, made his move towards Anderson. Anderson had now turned toward the cat to assess the threat. Anderson started backpedaling; the cougar did exactly what nature told it to do. Just as you'd expect, it charged Anderson, leaping into his chest and knocking both of them to the ground, with Anderson on his back.

However, Anderson, who was a jujitsu fan and a follower of mixed martial arts, had a move up his sleeve called The Guard. Finding the cougar's waist much thinner than a human opponent, Anderson quickly wrapped his legs around the cougar's abdomen and rolled the cougar over onto its back. Anderson had reversed The Guard and was now in The Mount, a position that put him on top of the big cat. From this position, Anderson was looking down the muzzle of inch-long fangs, claw-laden paws and millions of years of predatory genetics. Anderson possessed neither fangs nor claws, but he did have a cerebral cortex superior to the cougar. Anderson grabbed the cougar's throat, driving his thumbs into where he knew the carotid arteries were on a human and believed them to be on a cougar. Leaning in and splaying out his elbows, he pinned the cougar's claws back away from his body and face as he continued the strangulation. For the next 2-1/2 minutes Anderson would apply his choke to the cougar. The cougar for lack of grip, or Anderson's inability to find the arteries, lapsed in and out of consciousness, making no noise but continuing to intermittently wiggle.

By proximity or adjusting grip Anderson got his thumb in the cougar's mouth. The cougar, using its powerful jaws, crushed his thumb. This forced Anderson to let go of the cougar's throat. With its throat now freed, the big cat instantly began slashing at Anderson with its claws like a heavyweight boxer working a speed bag. The majority of the cat's strikes slashed at Anderson's heavy sweatshirt and only struck his chest a few times. Having lost the advantage, Anderson separated explosively from the cat. Without hesitation, Anderson then turned and ran away. Anderson's purpose for running was twofold: first, to escape and second, to run to his van where he retrieved a baseball bat. Anderson immediately returned to the site of his confrontation with full intention of killing the cougar by beating it to death. Instead of taking off as Anderson had done, the cougar had in fact, lingered. It was still looking for food, which it found in Anderson's bag of four peanut butter and jelly sandwiches.

Anderson, for his part, had wrestled in college and enjoyed the then-new Ultimate Fighting Championship (UFC) television broadcasts. The unique thing that Anderson did in preparation for his hand-to-hand combat with the cougar was that he had spent a good amount of time wrestling with a 120-pound German Shepherd named Forrest. During one winter while unemployed, Anderson had decided to try his ultimate fighting techniques and his jujitsu on a dog. Little did he know this unusual activity would come in so handy.

To add a piece of absurdity to the incident, the local park ranger noted that the trail that Anderson was riding on did not allow bikes. The fine for having a bike on the path was $50. The Ranger, however, decided not to cite Anderson, saying that he thought the cougar was his warning.

Source: The Peninsula Daily News, Mike Dawson, Sunday, May 26, 1996

Time

Time is critical. The longer you are in contact with a predator the lower your chances of success. The reason is simple; the predators chose you; you didn't choose. They chose you because you have something they want; your money or your meat. Further, the predators have weighed the moment and decided they can win the day; they can take from you what they want.

Distance

Keeping distance from a predator is a great policy. The farther away you are from having contact with a predator, the better off you are, as they are less likely to chose you. Think of it in the context of the cougar and Phil Anderson. When Anderson saw the cougar, he tried to get distance by backpedaling, albeit unsuccessfully. Distance is your friend and an impediment to predators executing their plans.

The more distance between you and a suspicious person, the better for you.

Exposure

Exposure is a simple and yet ruthless concept. In the wilderness exposure kills you. Exposure is uncomfortable emotionally; As being exposed can be embarrassing. Exposure to a predator can be a serious threat to your health. Exposing your body to the claws of a cougar most assuredly will leave you with the wounds that Anderson sustained. Distance will limit exposure. If you sense a criminal element you are lucky, because criminals generally make every effort to conceal themselves and their intent. Take our advice – heed your inner voice. If you feel threatened, don't exposure yourself. If you are at party and things start to go awry, leave. If a person makes you feel creepy, get away from them. If you are threatened do not expose yourself. Get in your car, walk away, or get on the next train, even if it is not going to your intended destination.

Coyotes

The smallest of the major predators is the coyote. Oddly though, they are a predator that has flourished in the face of mankind's incursion into the natural world and our changing of the environment.

Unlike the big cats, which rely on stealth and ambush; bears, which rely on strength; or wolves, which go after large game as a group, coyotes specialize in attacking the small and weak. While there are similarities between wolves and coyotes, wolves often take on deer, elk, and on occasion, moose. Coyotes by comparison would be more interested in something wounded, or too young and inexperienced to get away from its attacker. Coyotes also favor the slow and ponderous if those prey animals don't have too much of a defense. Unless they're going for very small prey like moles or mice, they will attack in packs, using distraction and numbers to bring down what they are hunting.

The human form of coyote behavior follows the same strategy, relying more on trickery and numbers than strength.

Mrs. X, that is what we are going to call her, and we are going to obfuscate some facts as well, because when we finish Mrs. X is going be painted in a very unflattering light.

Mrs. X found her 20 pound dog being attacked by coyotes. Coyotes are clever and they have figured out that the dogs that they attack in the subdivision will not run very far, the electronic invisible fence is the reason dogs don't run very far. Once a dog wanders from a yard in which an invisible fence has been installed, the dog receives a small electrical shock from its collar. The dog faces painful disciplinary action if it leaves the yard. In this case, the dog was twelve years old. As we know, for most dog breeds that's an elderly animal. Now you have a dog that will not run to far because of the invisible fence, cannot run quickly due to age, is just the right size for a good meal for a couple of coyotes, and is not protected by a fence. Yes, fences are designed to keep things out of your yard as well as in.

Mrs. X was able to scare the coyotes away, and saving her dog, by yelling at them.

Here is the untold story. Mrs. X revealed that she, too, is well trained, just like her dog. She stated, (and this is a paraphrase of her statement), "I don't like the idea that there have not been enough warnings for us dog owners to alert us to these issues." She is trained to believe that everything is OK, and if it not, the authorities will be sure and go out of their way to tell her. The fact is, she has set her dog up for attack by training the dog that it cannot run beyond a certain point. Mrs. X takes no responsibility to understand her environment, and then swiftly passes the blame on to the authorities.

Further, the city where she resides has a website that makes a point to inform people that they should keep an eye out for coyotes, but Mrs. X thinks that more should be done.

We would say that lack of insight, lack of effort, and lack of responsibility on the part of the dog owner makes for an easy target. No website, or authority is going to save every animal from the opportunistic predator, such as a coyotes, it is simply impossible.

If you abdicate your responsibility to protect yourself and your loved ones then you will find yourself as lost and set up for an opportunistic predator as Mrs. X and her dog.

Here is what you can do to avoid the opportunistic predator:

1. Take responsibility for your own safety. Do not assign that responsibility to others with the assumption that all will be just fine. All you need to do is look at the ratio of police to the civilian population and you can see that you are likely to be on your own in the event of an emergency. According to the U.S. Department of Justice, Bureau of Justice Statistics, currently on average the ratio of police is about 2.3 officers per 1,000 civilians. That is an aggregate across the U.S. In some rural areas the ratio is higher and in some cities lower. Nonetheless, the point is made.

2. Take a moment and see where you are on the spectrum of victimization. To the predator the world looks like a herd of sheep, the weakest – usually the youngest, elderly, or ill – are most likely to be attacked. – See Mrs. X's elderly dog.

3. Once you know where you are on the spectrum of victimization, act accordingly. Use preventive measures. Here is a tip sheet you can use:

Home

1. When you move into a new place, change the locks. Predators like easy entrance especially into a space with which they are familiar.

2. Put deadbolt locks on all doors leading outside. Make it harder for the criminal to get what they want, make a criminal burn calories. The more calories they see they have to burn the more likely they are to move on.

3. Double-check your windows and doors every time you leave home to make sure they're locked, especially during summer months when windows and doors are open often. Again, an unlocked door or an open window is just the invitation a human coyote is looking for.

4. Keep your curtains or blinds drawn when you are not home. Predators are not inclined to waste time guessing whether there is something good inside, they prefer to know their efforts are going to bring results.

The door is open, it was locked when you left.

5. Install a door scope in your front door, one with a wide sweep and don't open the door until you have seen who is at the door. Vision, seeing them before they see you, is the most basic of the defense systems.

6. Require repair people to show I.D. before you open the door. Know who is in your home and make them prove they are who they say they are.

7. If you are in the home and a burglar enters, escape if you can. This is a situation best dealt with by getting distance and letting the police handle the situation. No animal is going to stay and fight if they, or their offspring, are not in danger – you should adopt this rule.

8. If you come home and suspect somebody is in your home, don't enter, just call the police.

Walking

1. Avoid walking alone. Unless you are the alpha predator and you know it, groups and numbers add strength.

2. Stay in lit areas, no short cut is worth the loss of life. Predators don't want to be seen, stay in the light.

3. Walk in the middle of sidewalks and walk facing traffic. This makes it harder for a car to come up behind you. Most predators prefer surprise, don't let them speed up behind you.

4. If you feel threatened, go right back to where you came, Whether The store, apartment, bar, or wherever. It is a known path and you can trace it quickly.

5. If you have finished shopping, don't sit in your car and check your purchases. Wait until you get home. Displaying your goods in the middle of the predator's hunting ground is foolish.

Driving

1. Never pick up hitchhikers. Inviting a potential predator into a locked steel tube with you makes no sense.

2. Keep your doors locked. Remember, fences keep things in and out – locks do the same.

3. Keep your gas tank filled. Being stranded is not a good thing and when you are stressed you will make bad choices and take risks you normally would not take.

4. If you are being followed, drive immediately to a fire or police station. Human predators hate the idea of bigger, stronger, more prepared people getting in the way of their intentions.

5. If you are bumped in the rear of your car by the car behind you, stay in your vehicle. This is a tactic, a trick, to get you out of your car. This is a ruse, a trick to get you out of the safety of your car and available for assault. If you can drive to a public place to assess the situation, do it.

6. Do not use an ATM after dark. The situation is simply too good of a hunting ground.

Exercise 1: 360-degree head scan

In his book, *101 Ultralight Backpacking Tips,* author Mike McClelland introduces the LATS system for weather prediction in the outdoors. LATS is an acronym for *Look At The Sky.* However, for our purposes we are going to use the LAYO system, which stands for *Look Around You Often.*

LAYO - Look around you often.

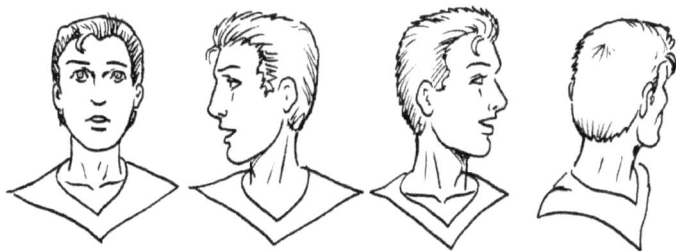

While you don't want to look like you are constantly moving your head, practice doing a regular sweep from side to side and behind (and every so often above). Try to actually see what you are looking at rather than just glossing over what is around you.

In learning the art of tracking, trackers often get so intent on tracking the trail of signs and footprints that they tune out everything but the ground in front of them. For man-trackers such as those employed by law enforcement or Search and Rescue, this can be a very bad idea. Off to the side, or at the edges of our vision can be anything from a lost hiker's windbreaker to an escaped fugitive. With regard to the lost hiker, it may mean missing a valuable clue in the midst of a large wild area; for a fugitive being tracked, it gives the pursued the opportunity to take out the person most likely to follow his trail.

Wilderness Awareness School founder and author Jon Young found that the young trackers he was mentoring in his Shikari Tracking Guild program often fell into this trap, so he formalized a series of movements to be performed every 50 feet or so. The tracker would look up, scan from forward to 90 degrees left, and then slowly scan back to 90 degrees right. Next would be a slow turn of the head (and body) 180 degrees behind, holding for at least 20 seconds. Then, the student would do a 180-degree arc above their head to make sure there were no creatures of interest above them. It sounds kind of crazy to make such a simple thing into a formalized "ritual", but the point wasn't just to see what was going on in a 360-degree arc. It was to make such scanning second nature, to make the behavior an almost unconscious habit. For our purposes though we need to adapt that practice to suit a more urban venue. This means that we might need to relax the exercise a little, to keep the head moving rather than, "look and stop, look and stop."

Exercise 1-A: Go to your local park and take a stroll.

Start out walking slowly and do the above steps as described, only look around every set of ten steps rather than every 50 feet (you can probably do the vertical scan on a more intermittent basis… or not. It's up to you.). Make an effort to not only look, but take the time to really see what is in your view. Most people give what's around them a cursory glance without looking for subtleties or causalities. You can do better. Ask internal questions about what you see. "Why is that couple walking ten feet apart?" "Why is that man watching everyone that goes by?" "Is that large dog running free owner-less or does he belong to one of the people within my line of sight?" "Why did all of those birds just fly out of that bush?"

Another idea is to narrate what you see (to yourself please, the idea is not to make yourself stand out) as if describing the walk to an audience that has never been there. This can make you take more of an interest in what is going on around you, and might make you pay better attention to why things are happening as they are.

Sometimes trouble is easy to spot, if you have your mind in the here and now when needed.

Exercise 1-B: Take it downtown

Practicing on a busy downtown street during the workweek takes the experience up a notch. The sidewalks are often crowded, and people are in proximity to you all the time. You might feel uncomfortable looking around, as many people in the city avoid eye contact at all costs. While we certainly don't recommend "eyeballin" strangers on the street, you can let your eyes wander past them as you look around. The flow of foot traffic might be fast enough that you feel you can't do more than a glance behind you. Just move over to a wall, lean against it for a moment, and scan the crowd as if you lost your friend. Anyone coming up on you? Anyone "eyeballin" you? Is anything disrupting the human river flowing past you?

In the end. The objective is to make looking around an unconscious habit that requires little drain on your conscious attention, until something comes into your view that seems out of place or threatening.

Not to beat a dead horse, but cutting off your own senses in public is a VERY bad idea.

Chapter Six
You are a Resource:
How you make yourself a resource

"Civilization as it is known today could not have evolved, nor can it survive, without an adequate food supply."

–Norman Borlaug

The Whistler Resort is located in southern British Columbia, Canada. Whistler is the destination point for all kinds of recreation, although predominantly skiing, with over 8,000 acres of skiable slope, mountain bike trails, and lakes. Whistler, with its central village, even hosted winter events for the 2010 Vancouver Olympics. Built-up, popular, urban and full of all the modern amenities, it is a destination for people from around the world to enjoy outdoor sports with modern conveniences. One of those modern conveniences is the outdoor hot tub. In June of 2012, what would be considered the off-season for the Whistler Resort, a 55-year-old man from British Columbia took advantage of lower rates and a beautiful cool summer evening. Slipping into the outside hot tub the Canadian man began to relax into what most of us would consider a perfect end to the day. His evening was going to take an extraordinary change, however; a meeting of two worlds that he had not anticipated.

As the jets bubbled and the hot tub motor churned away, the man found himself lurching forward in the hot tub from a heavy blow to the back of the head. Shocked and still conscious the man spun around in the hot tub to see what had struck him so hard in the back of the head. Standing on the edge of the hot tub on the deck was a North American black bear. The only thing separating the two was the warm bubbling water, a poor defense. The man struck out with his best defense. He yelled the top of his lungs at the bear, jumped out of the tub and bolted for the safety of the inside of the condominium. The police responded quickly to the report of a man being attacked by a bear, and arriving at the scene of the hot tub attack, sent the man to the Whistler Healthcare Center for treatment for the lacerations to the back of his head. A bear claw can leave awful lacerations because, well, that is what they're designed to do. A quick search of the surrounding area found the bear, and it was shot and killed. The bear had a necropsy performed to see if there is a determination for the attack, such as rabies.

The need for situational awareness should never be underestimated, even when you are in a "safe" location.

One of the interesting things about this attack of the bear on the human is the placement of the eyes. As we discussed earlier, eye placement indicates whether an animal is a predator or a grazer. There is a story that illustrates the idea of innate preparation – preparation for the environment and the context in which animals, or people, operate. The story goes like this. A local guy had a wife that was what could be called a "crazy cat lady." That is to say, she had a lot cats. The husband was not a great fan of cats but nonetheless indulged her desire. One day he and the neighbor were out on the front porch when one of the cats strolled across the lawn and into the stubble of the freshly cut alfalfa field, no doubt looking for mice.

As the story goes the two men sat and watched the cat begin the hunt. Then, swooping down out of the sky at about a 30° angle came a dark blur; it was a hawk. The hawk crashed into the cat, pinned it to the ground, and within a second was back in the air with the cat in its talons. The man looked at his neighbor friend and said, "Well, nine to go." True or not, the story illustrates the fact that the house cat came from the environment of the house, a place of complete safety. It was the alpha predator who was fed on a daily basis and only hunted because it had to via instinct. Add to that a very simple mechanical orientation of forward set eyes used for stereoscopic vision and perdition. It is very unlikely that the cat ever saw the hawk descending on it. Also it is highly unlikely that the concept of a predator from above, let alone out of the sky, even entered into the cat's thought process. Add to this the fact that it is more than likely that the hawk attacked the cat from its blind spot, and you find yourself looking at a combination of information that shows that the cat was easier prey than a rabbit.

A cat easier prey than a rabbit?

Yes, the rabbit has wide-placed eyes, which give it a wider scope of vision such that the rabbit is almost able to see completely behind itself. A rabbit also has larger ears to hear the surrounding environment better, and fur the color of the indigenous grasses and topography. If we were to place the same two animals, a cat and a rabbit, in a life-threatening situation once again, but in this instance with a threat that comes from the land instead of the sky, and is in the form of a coyote you'll find once again that one of the animals is designed to deal with predators and the other is a smaller predator not designed to confront larger versions of its own behavior.

This is how it would work. Coyotes will hunt in a pack. The pack is designed to confuse the animal being attacked, tire it out, and through fatigue and stealth close on the victim to strike the killing blow, most likely again from the rear. Using the information from the previous scenario it is easy to predict the probable outcome of a coyote versus a house cats, the cat becomes food. The rabbit, on the other hand, while it has the potential to become food it is better suited to the environment. The eyes and ears of a rabbit are designed to give early warning and its coloring to make it hard for predators to detect it.

The hawk making a fast meal of the house cat is an example of a cross-platform predation, from the sky to land. The coyotes and cats are an example of lateral, or same platform, predation. There are other forms of cross-platform predation such as the polar bear staring into a hole in the ice. The hole is where seals enter and leave the water, and the polar bear stands over the hole waiting for the unsuspecting seal to surface for air where the attack can take place.

Killer whales use beaching, a technique of using the surf and a lunge forward to launch themselves on the beach, hence the name. They do this to strike at the seals, which believe that making it to the beach, or land, will protect them from the watery hunting ground of the killer whale only to find the intelligent predator has developed a technique to cross platforms and gain a quick meal.

Predators will cross platforms to get the resources they need. But, more importantly, if you cross into their domain you will find yourself unprepared, unaware and an easy victim.

The cat that was eaten by the hawk believed it was safe. It did so because all of its experience in life indicated it was. The man who was hit by the bear? He believed he was safe because he was in a hot tub, but the hot tub was pushed up onto the edge of the bear's environment.

You might think that making yourself a resource for the human predator is a stupid thing to do, but often it's not a matter of conscious choice, it's a matter of inattention. You are probably aware of the discussion around the dangers of texting and even talking while driving a heavy motor vehicle; but similar dangers lurk when you are a pedestrian, riding public transportation, zooming along on a bike or any number of non-vehicular venues. The root problem, again, is being unaware.

Living in a country where we are somewhat insulated from personal violence (depending on who we are), we tend to become complacent about danger. Because of this, we sometimes do half the work for the people who would harm us.

It's not that easy being a modern human sometimes. Our lives are a lot more complicated than when all we had to worry about was keeping warm and killing bison for food. We spend a lot of time in our heads these days, mulling over everything that troubles us or even caught up in things that are wonderful for us to contemplate. But when we are in our heads thinking there is one thing we're not thinking of, the here and now. Human predators like this, a lot.

A resource for a human predator is much like a resource for an animal predator, someone that can be taken down with a minimum of risk and effort. Unfortunately, modern society reinforces this trait in many of us.

With all the things to get lost in the corridors of our mind, we now have numerous external attention thieves, most of them electronic. Music players, smartphones, tablets, text messaging, etc., all draw our attention to a small area for however long it takes for our need for E-activity to be satisfied. What better time for a predator to harvest.

At the very least, slaves to their electronic masters should take a lesson from Exercise One and carefully scrutinize the area before letting their attention be stolen. Be alert. Whatever the distraction, it can probably be handled just as well from home, a restaurant or a coffee shop than from a vulnerable place. Wait for a safe place to engage in these behaviors to avoid being a resource to scum.

Cut from the herd

In almost every predator encounter, the prey is cut off from any assistance by being driven into isolation by the predator. Sometimes, prey will be taken in such a manner that its companions flee, but more often an animal is cut from the herd and driven or tricked into isolation. Then, when tired or wounded enough, the prey becomes someone's resource (meal).

Humans are thinking animals, with a sense of possible futures, but we too can be "cut from the herd." A human predator wants as little in the way of witnesses or possible good Samaritan help as possible. To do this they require their prey to be someplace away from prying eyes. Only the most deranged attack in full view of the public herd. Instead of the tall grass, human predators often rely on trickery.

Straggling behind your group, never a good idea.

You should always be wary when approached by someone you've never met who is being especially friendly. Most people have a certain reserve when approaching strangers. When a stranger is suddenly treating you like you're the most interesting person around, you should likely go to yellow alert (cautious, but not hostile). The person could be someone proselytizing their church, selling Cub Scout raffle tickets or wanting to sell you a timeshare condo. The person could also be someone distracting you so their associate can pick your pocket or purse, or worse yet, knocking you over the head to drag you into a car or alley. (This is where Exercise 1 (360-degree head scan) can come in handy *if* you feel comfortable looking away from the person in front of you for a moment).

Let's look at a few scenarios. Say you're a person of average attractiveness. Out of the blue, a very attractive person starts coming on to you in a big way. This is very flattering, and sexually stimulating and if legitimate, well, good for you. However, there's also the possibility that this attractive bait is being used to "cut you from the herd," to get you alone. How many men, throughout history have been led out the back way by an attractive female with the promise of a fun time, only to get their skull caved in at the end of a dark alley? How many women have been taken somewhere by that great guy they felt a connection with, only to find themselves surrounded by leering strangers bent on rape and worse?

This may sound paranoid; most people in the world are not out to get you, but enough uncaring bastards are out there to always warrant caution.

Body language can play a part in some encounters. If a stranger is coming up, all loosey goosey and smiling like a 100-watt bulb but never lets you see their hand, you might want to take it to red alert (ready to defend) before you let them get too close. That gorgeous, smiling girl who wants to show you something down the alley is possibly not going to show you what you want to see, unless you want to see her large boyfriend and his cronies holding crowbars and baseball bats.

The takeaway here is be cautious about letting a stranger get you someplace isolated, no matter how friendly they seem. People who turn the charm on high immediately usually want something. It may be your vote in an upcoming election, it maybe the wallet you're carrying or it may be your life.

Not looking like a resource

In our modern society, we are driven to keep up a certain image whether that image is truly who we are or not. It seems part of the human psyche to "show off our plumage," only in the case of humans that usually means either a great body or wealth.

We are often amazed at people driving 60 thousand dollar cars, not because they are particularly useful, but simply because being the owner of one confers status on the owner. It's the same with having a Gucci bag or a Rolex on your wrist. These may be symbols of wealth and perfectly acceptable in context, such as in a swanky restaurant or at a board meeting but the same status symbols, when carried out in the general public, often generate avarice.

There is a time and place for everything. If you feel the need to make an ostentatious display, you should strongly consider limiting your showing off to appropriate venues. Wandering around showing

The predator often chooses the more lucrative looking target. The more expensive the clothes, the more enticing.

off your wealth will garner a variety of reactions. Average people may be put off (and perhaps a little jealous) but the human predator may start to salivate and plan mischief. Think about it. Say you're a criminal working in a park and two people pull up to the parking lot, both intent on taking a walk. Are you going to follow the guy from the Honda civic dressed in sweats from JC Penney and wearing a Timex or the guy in the tailored tracksuit who emerged from the brand new Lexus SUV with a Rolex on his wrist? There's nothing wrong with being wealthy, but showing it should presume some careful thought on when such displays are wise.

Besides wealth as an attraction for predators to single out a person, attitude and awareness are also attributes to be considered. We think we've already hammered home the dangers of being unaware, but how about how we carry ourselves?

In the animal world, the weak and the young are usually the first targets of the predators. The human world is often not that different.

Some people think that because they are not rich that they're immune to being attacked. We assure you that there are far too many addicts out there that are willing to do harm to you for anything they can sell to get set up. It is stupid to assume you are immune from attack for any reason.

"Predator for a Day" Drill

This exercise is not complicated. It involves going downtown, or to some very pedestrian-oriented area (mall, sporting event, park, etc.), finding a nice unobtrusive spot and watching your fellow human beings with "evil" intent. Please keep in mind that this is a training sortie; don't get carried away!

A good place to sit is a coffee shop with a clear view of passers by. Take a notebook and pen with you, to take notes on what you notice (journaling) and camouflage your intentions, taking a keen interest in strangers makes them nervous, and you, just like your criminal counterpart, do not want to draw attention to yourself.

Now, observe.

Being a faux predator, what are you looking for? You want an easy target, someone who will not give you much trouble, and who will be unlikely to see it coming until too late. You certainly would want to avoid anyone who looks like they could be trouble. Certainly there are predators who are out to prove something, but not the ones who want to stay out of jail.

As people pass, perhaps you would see someone walking along in a fearful manner, displaying body language that screams, "I'm afraid!" If robbery were your intent, this might be the person to follow, and if you could isolate them, you might be able to get what you want with a minimum of effort. Another person passing may be totally living in their own world, possibly having an internal conversation with someone they want to tell off and being oblivious to the here and now. Such a person might never realize there was any danger; they'd never see it coming till it was too late.

Who in the crowd is strong? Who is weak? Who is aware and who has blocked their attention with preoccupation or electronic devices? Is anyone cutting through pathways that might be a good ambush site? What kind of clothing are they wearing and will it interfere with your attack? Might they be armed? How do they move? Clumsily? Carefully or gracefully? Do they appear to be wealthy? Would a crime provide a big payoff?

You can peel these questions back like the layers of an onion and keep finding more. Don't be constrained to thinking only about the items listed here. Think of the things that you see on your own. Just don't go all "Dark Side" and start freaking people out. That is not the purpose here and it would be counter productive.

After you have gleaned all that you can from this, switch the exercise around and come back to the light. Imagine yourself an undercover crime fighter, and observe, looking for lions in the grass rather than the sheep in the field. Look for anyone who might be dangerous, anyone who might be watching with a predatory look in his or her eye. Also look for anyone who might be a danger by way of mental impairment, drunkenness, drug use or just plain shouldn't be out on the streets. You don't necessarily have to be a criminal to be dangerous.

Take your notes home, and think about what you've seen. The act of observing makes you a more natural observer. Let's say you are looking at your iPhone while crossing the street Yes, the crosswalk

Our modern plugged-in lifestyle, does little to enhance our awareness of what's happening around us.

indicates you are in a designated walking zone, but someone driving a car, also on his iPhone doesn't see the crossing paint and hits you. One environment, the one of rules and codes, meets the immutable laws of nature.

Being in a car and finding yourself in the wrong neighborhood, is the equivalent of the British Columbian man in his hot tub. It is important that you are able to assess your environment, to know that the context of your space has changed and to respect that change of environment.

Animals can't afford to not pay attention

In one of his many talks on nature awareness, author Jon Young discussed who in the animal world is most likely to die once leaving the care of its parents. Though there is often a very high mortality rate amongst any juvenile animals, once grown, it is the yearlings that are most often removed from the gene pool.

There are many reasons for this, most of them boil down to lack of experience or skill. In young predators, it's the lack of hunting success that often kills (which is why many attacks on humans come from young animals that are not succeeding at hunting wild prey). For prey animals, which derive most of their food from plants, the main killer is lack of awareness skills. The old "mossback" buck has lived a very long lifetime for a deer because he is constantly scanning without having to work at it. His experience allows him to use intermittent awareness. The yearlings on the other hand indulge in juvenile be-havior that leaves them following their immediate needs with gusto while not paying attention to the big picture of their surroundings. If they can pass through this phase and not be killed, they will learn to pay attention and their chances for avoiding being killed by a preda-tor go up as their experience increases.

It is fairly easy to see similarities in the human world. Extreme sports notwithstanding, most people learn to be careful of their bodies as they age. Unfortunately, many remain stuck in adolescence when it comes to awareness. In general, we are not daily on some-one's menu and the majority of us may never come in contact with a predator, two-legged or four-legged. This insulation, while providing the illusion of security, does little to help people learn to be watchful.

The changes in the environment can be the change from day to night. Simply put, night provides cover. Change in the number of people, from few to many, or vice versa. Some predators, such as sexual predators want no witnesses and the one-on-one control. Some, such as teenagers prefer to work in the power of groups.

Animals Use Constant Intermittent Awareness

The animals of the forest, for all their pastoral beauty, live a day-to-day existence based primarily on two things; eat enough and don't be eaten. Even the largest predators, while not generally being in danger from other predators, still have to watch out for bigger and badder versions of themselves.

Every creature of the wild must have a higher degree of awareness than, say, Uncle Marvin, who rarely moves from the couch other than to make nachos or get new batteries for the remote. You'd think that these animals would live in a constant state of nervous semi-frenzy trying to see, smell and hear everything that might come after them, right? Not so much.

To live in a constant state of nervous awareness is actually counter to survival. Animals use a variety of methods to avoid having to be "on" all the time. Watch a group of Canada geese, and you will see at least one with head up while the others feed. If that one gets agitated and starts vocalizing and pumping its head up and down, the whole group goes on alert. It's the same with a herd of deer. When one starts huffing or looking intently in one direction everyone starts looking in that direction, preparing to take off if needed. But when there is no discernible danger, animals relax, let their stress levels fall off and just… live. While you can't say this strategy is 100% successful or there would be no predators left in the forest. The opposite would leave these creatures so stressed that their lives would be very short anyway.

Aside from having lookouts, how do animals remain aware enough to live to reproduce? They use intermittent awareness. It works like this. As you probably know, animals have strong senses of smell and hearing (sight also, but in dense woods, sight is often the least of the senses used). Rather than constantly sniffing like a bloodhound, a deer will let the scents of the forest come to it on the breeze. When something comes that smells threatening, then things go to Defcon 2.

The forest has its own alarm systems if one knows what one is listening for. Here's an example. A human wanders along a trail huffing under a heavy pack and making little attempt to be stealthy. She sees a robin along the trail but thinks little of it even though that robin may be exhibiting behavior that asks to be noticed and not intruded on. Our hiker, having no real training in that sort of thing, ignores the signs. The robin flies up to a high perch, not so much afraid as irritated to be treated so rudely, and loudly complains with alarm calls shrill and piercing. The Pacific wren hears this and begins its own little alarm, "chip,… chip!" and this alerts the juncos. The juncos alert the towhee and the deer, a quarter mile away, hears all this commotion and quietly fades back into the brush. A few minutes later, the hiker walks right by where the animal was feeding, seeing nothing. The deer watches her pass from the brush.

If the deer was constantly waiting for danger to rear its ugly head it would, as the great tracker Tom Brown Jr. once said, "…be the size of a shivery Chihuahua."

Instead, the deer's honed senses recognize certain patterns and those patterns alert it to upcoming danger. This is what we want to learn in our own danger avoidance routines, to be alerted by cues, not spending every minute being afraid of being attacked.

The Brain, Patterns and Alertness

A healthy brain, one not tired, on drugs, or otherwise disturbed makes up lies. Your brain lies to you on a daily and on a moment-by-moment basis. The brain's lies are well meant, done in the good hearted attempt to keep you from going insane. If your brain did not reject much of the information that the senses bring into your nervous system you would be completely dysfunctional. The onslaught of information would be a sensory tidal wave crashing and crushing your ability to make order of the world. The brain goes through a process that might be described like this. It says, "I recognize that, it's a chair, it's in the other room – not important." The brain recognizes the pattern of the chair sitting at its appointed place in another room, right where it is supposed to be. Recognizing the chair, the brain, on a subconscious level, chooses not to push it forward to your conscious mind. It also makes the same choices regarding such things as the table, the flowers on the table, the vase holding the flowers, or the picture on the wall. You can see how all of this adds up very quickly. The brain has existing information, and makes general assumptions of environment based on this existing information and it adheres to those assumptions until otherwise needed. These general assumptions, the recognition of known patterns, and the quick dismissal of extraneous information are how the brain makes up lies.

If you've ever traveled to another country, experienced another culture, you may be inclined to say, "I loved Japan; it was wonderful." Part of that wonderfulness is that things are different, yet the fundamental patterns remain similar. Think of it this way; the Tokyo subway system is complex, multilayered, and busy. The New York subway system is complex, multilayered, and busy. Say you had grown up in New York. You would be familiar with the New York subway system, and when in Japan you would have a general idea of how the Japanese system works, how the tickets are purchased and where to stand safely.

However, what you'll also find is that the queues for lining up are different. The signage, while it will be placed in similar places, will look completely different. This similar, yet slightly different, experience titillates some people, and for others it creates frustration. Regardless, the patterns are similar. This creates a sense of awareness in the mind and the need for a level of alertness not called upon in your normal day-to-day life. This high level of awareness can be exhausting. You've no doubt experienced this when you move to a new city, or traveled for pleasure. You can become quite tired at the end of the day because of all the extra mental effort.

The Stroop Effect

In 1935, John Ridley Stroop discovered that if he printed the name of a color in a different color than the written name of the color the human mind would choose the written word over the actual color in which the word was written. It works better with a series of words and in color instead of black and white, but we are going to try to attempt to create the effect here. Look at the word below and say the color in which the word is written.

BLACK

More than likely you responded with "black" when in fact the question you were asked was, "Say the name of the color in which the word black is written," which is, of course, gray.

This demonstrates several things, but the thing that we would like you to focus on is that your mind defaulted to the written word, and the written word is pattern. Pattern recognition is the key to intermittent attentiveness.

Now having chosen the word black over the color gray in your response might be considered a failure. In fact, in the context of the question asked, it was. In the context of the real world, however, this is your brain performing precisely as nature intended.

In nature many animals, such as dogs or deer, are colorblind. Color is not necessary for their survival. However, pattern recognition is literally the difference between life and death. Now clearly, shades of gray, light, dark, and shadows, all of these play into their method of pattern recognition, but true color vision is not necessary for their survival. Nature has also buried brain pattern recognition deep in the human brain. So for our purposes and the way nature intended, you did not fail the test. In fact, the Stroop effect has demonstrated just how important pattern recognition is to intermittent awareness.

Let us go back to the example of the chair in the adjacent room that we used earlier. As long as that chair remains on the ground sitting next to the table the pattern is correct. Your brain at a subconscious level simply acknowledges that all things are correct from your sense of experience and the chair is of no consequence. However, if the chair has been thrown through the air at you by an attacker the chair now breaks a known pattern. This breaking of a known pattern requires your immediate attention. After having dodged the chair, let us take you into another room away from the incident. We now need you to describe the chair that was thrown at you. The only way you are likely to describe it well is if you are already familiar with the chair. Perhaps it was from a dining room set that your grandmother had owned and had bequeathed to you. You are intimate with this chair because you have sat on it since you were a child. Otherwise, you will unlikely be able to tell us how many dowels there are in the back of the chair or that those painted dowels contrast with the natural wood color of the seat. The breaking of the pattern was important for your safety.

Animals use movement, and specifically a movement that violates any known and accepted pattern, as a flag that there may be a threat. You have this same skill innate in your brain just as the Stroop Effect has demonstrated in our little test.

"Odd One Out" Drill

This is a simple drill you can use to sharpen your pattern recognition skills and wind it tightly around intermittent awareness when it comes to human predators. It's based on the old Sesame Street game, accompanied by a song, called, "One of these things is not like the others." As you may recall the song asked the question, "Can you tell which thing is not like the others?" For example, a series of shapes would begin to fill the television screen, a square, followed by another square, followed by another square, followed by a triangle. Basic, sure, but you get the premise.

Find a group of people. Because of people's tendency to select common traits and behaviors, it's likely that they will be dressed similarly. One or maybe two individuals will exhibit a slight variation from this norm. They will be different from the rest, thus disrupting the pattern. This disruption could indicate group dominance, or group subservience. On one end of the scale, the dominant individual may

LAYO. A pattern disruption usually has a reason.

adopt clothing that shows, say, through pattern that they are of the group, yet different, and in a dominant fashion. The same goes in reverse, dress behaviors may indicate a subservient role. Your drill is to find one or both of those individuals in the group that you have decided to observe. Once you have determined that they fit one of these roles ask yourself the question, "What three things lead me to this conclusion?" Often we do this during the course of the day, but we don't consciously seek the disruptions and patterns that give us these indicators. We are asking you, like any animal in the wild, or good poker player, to find those tells and consciously make note of them.

Chapter Seven
Know the Hunter

"The ancient feud between cat and dog is not forgotten in the north, for the Lynx is the deadly foe of the Fox and habitually kills it when there is soft snow and scarcity of easier prey."

-Ernest Thompson Seton

It is kind of an odd thing to be human. At one time, we were a part of nature, subject to the same rules as the rest of the natural world. Our ability to reason has helped us to make secure homes, our own dens of safety, with which we can block out the rest of the world. That security is not without cost, however. Most of us tend to assume that things, happening a certain way will continue to happen that way. We aren't prepared for change unless it happens slowly and gradually, giving us time to adjust. Sudden change for most humans is quite stressful.

It is that lack of belief in change that often leads us down the path of false security. If someone goes out to their driveway each morning, sipping coffee, enters their commuting car, then drives to work without incident, that is what will continue to happen in perpetuity, isn't it?

Not necessarily.

These are the ruts, the patterns that we carve into our psyches. Most of us are creatures of habit and as we do something enough times, we need less and less of our concentration to do it. You'd think this would free up "run time" for things like increased awareness and being in the moment, but it doesn't seem to work that way. Generally, this increased automatic competence allows us to daydream, have conversations with ourselves, or to stress about our problems. We rarely take note of what is around us unless we train ourselves to do so. Add to this such modern conveniences as music players, smart phones, etc., and half the time our attention is locked into a screen slightly larger than a business card.

Unfortunately, this is perfect for those who might prey on us. The next time you leave your house, try a day of pretending that someone is out to ambush you, pretend that you must be completely on your guard from sneak attack throughout the day (see the drill below). Notice any time that your attention lapses, and see if that would have been enough time for your invisible enemy to kill you. Some people might have trouble with this role play, but one thing in the human condition's arsenal is imagination and it's not a bad thing to keep it sharp as well as your awareness. At the end of the day you can tally how many times people got close to you before you noticed them and how many times you were subsequently 'killed.' Then, review the day and ask yourself how much more aware you were than usual.

The Dicta Boelcke

On October 28th, 1916, German Ace fighter pilot Oswald Boelcke died in a crash landing. At age 25, he left behind 40 aerial combat victories and something called "The Dicta Boelcke." The Dicta Boelcke was Boelcke's (pronounce Bowl-ka) eight-point treatise on air combat. You may not have heard of Oswald Boelcke, but you have probably heard of Manfred von Richthofen AKA The Red Baron, for whom Boelcke served as a mentor. Boelcke transferred the basic concepts of animal predator behavior, refined it and put in the air. We are going to bring the Dicta Boelcke down out of the sky and onto the street. It is, in our opinion, one of the greatest manuscripts in its clarity and simplicity regarding how to be a predator. Below are the eight items from The Dicta Boelcke, followed by a little bit of explanation and instruction on how you are going to use them to increase your awareness of potential threats.

NUMBER ONE: Try to secure the upper hand before attacking. If possible, keep the sun behind you.

NUMBER TWO: Always continue with an attack you have begun.

NUMBER THREE: Open fire only at close range, and then only when the opponent is squarely in your sights.

NUMBER FOUR: You should always try to keep your eye on your opponent, and never let yourself be deceived by ruses.

NUMBER FIVE: In any type of attack, it is essential to assail your opponent from behind.

NUMBER SIX: If your opponent dives on you do not try to get around his attack, but fly to meet it.

NUMBER SEVEN: When over the enemy's lines, always remember your own line of retreat.

NUMBER EIGHT: Tips for squadrons: In principle, it is better to attack in groups of four or six. Avoid two aircraft attacking the same opponent.

Predators of the sky want the same thing predators of the street want. An easy kill.

Let us now break each of these down and make them useful for us.

Number One:

Try to secure the upper hand before attacking. If possible, keep the sun behind you.

The principle expressed here is straightforward. Use the environment to make it hard for your victim to see the attack. Now in Boelcke's world, we're talking 360° of open sky. When operating in your world, a potential attacker has only 180° of that sphere. One way to imagine this is to start on your left-hand side, move across the top of your head over to your right hand and where your hand touches the ground on your right side. Then move in a 360° circle, beginning in front and rotating a complete circle, then coming back around to your starting position. Further, there is an unlikelihood that there will be attack coming from above your head. Although people do get attacked by crows for being too close to their nest with hatchlings, it is unlikely that a big cat is going to leap from a tree limb and attack you in an urban environment. One of the few examples of humans operating from above the top of your head in a predatory fashion is the sniper. So now we can remove the top half of our dome of awareness.

This leaves us with a smaller area in which to sweep for potential attack. It is possible that predators could use the concept of keeping the sun behind to help blind you in their attack, but it is more than likely they are going to use another form of obfuscating your vision. The opposite of using the sun to blind your opponent is using darkness. Coming from the shadows, and further, coming from the shadows somewhere other than directly in front of you, clearly fulfills the first dictum in Boelcke's list.

How would this manifest in your daily life? Let's simply say that you step outside your front door, and in this instance, you have a few front steps and a little bit of lawn between you and your car parked out on the street. This situation presents potential attack from the left side or the right side, and the farther you get from your front door it opens up your backside, or (as we've learned in the clock principle) the six o'clock, to potential attack. Further, a person should take into account what is to the left and to the right is it open lawn, until the next neighbor's lawn, or are the lawn separated by a 6 foot tall

wooden fence?
Are there shrub-
beries, trees, or
anything else that
may obfuscate a
potential attack-
er's position get-
ting them closer
to you so that
they can attack ef-
fectively. Now this
may sound a little
paranoid, but it is
not, it simply is

The Clock Principle
(Watch your 6!)

an assessment of your environment. At this level, it is not something
that you have to walk around with on a daily basis but if you make
the assessment it will become resident in your thought process, and
you will begin to see when things are out of the ordinary and respond
if needed.

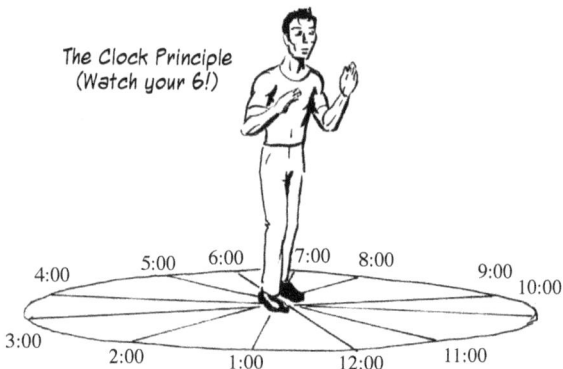

1. Distance

Keeping distance from an
area of obfuscation, such
as a tree, corner, hedge, car,
or dumpster creates space,
critical space, that predators
do not like. The more easily
they are seen, the less they
like it for one main reason;
the earlier you see them, the
more time you have to re-
spond. As predators formu-
late their attack, one of the
most important aspects of
the formula, is distance.

Keeping your distance from this guy
seems like a very good idea.

21 Foot Drill:
Distance Distance:
21 Feet is Your World.

Sergeant Dennis Tueller conducted a study, now called The Tueller Drill that showed that in a short-range attack, against a knife, that a person, or officer, needed 21 feet to get their gun drawn and defeat the attack. In other words, if you have a holstered gun and you intend to use it on an attacker rushing at you with a knife, if they are within 21 feet or less you get stabbed. The distance drill works this way. Step out your front door, and close the door. Now your rear is protected by the exterior walls of your home and the closed door. Next, beginning at a range of about three feet in front of your body (because that of course is where the predator needs to be to attack), look to each side in a sweeping motion, to the left and to the right, sweeping back and forth until you reach the magic 21 feet. Of course you will need to make an estimated guess as to what constitutes 21 feet.

21 feet may seem like a lot, but if someone is charging you with a knife, it will seem like inches.

2. Light
Boarders Drill: Light

Predators use the opposite of the blinding sun, the darkness of shadows and night, to make their actions unclear until they have secured the advantage of surprise. Your drill looks like this. The edge of light, as you can best perceive it is the same as with the 21-foot rule from The Tueller Drill. You need to stand and operate deep within the light, a streetlight if you like, but the edge of the light is the edge of danger. If when standing in the light you have less than 21 feet between you and the edge of the light, you are in the range for an explosive attack. One of the subsets of the first dictum is the idea of speed. It is not overly sophisticated, but it is immensely powerful if the victim is slower. The predators have checked that box, and if fairly sure that the opponent is slower than they are, they are then ready to attack the victim. If the victims have difficulty escaping or fighting because they are slower, they are lost. There is an adage that is popular in the anti-drug programs that "speed kills." Well the fact of the matter is it does, just not in the way the statement is intended to mean.

Another subset of this first dictum is the idea of surprise. Predators love surprise. Your job in this drill is to simply keep your attention to the areas where surprise can be used against you. The most straightforward way that you can avoid surprise is using the concept of distance. You need to keep distance from any place that you may sense an attack can come from. As we previously stated, and will state again, predators do not like light, nor open space. Make them cross open space and make them do it in the light. There is your simple, two-pronged defensive awareness tactic that you are to employ in this drill.

Number Two: Always continue with an attack you have begun.

This part of the Dicta comes from a simple idea. In World War I combat, when chivalry still existed, was that if a pilot appeared to be going down, the attack was cut off; the attacker stopped his attack. Unfortunately, what became common practice was for the pilot who appeared to be going down to fake that they had been severely damaged and were going down. This technique of faking severe damage became a ruse to make the attacker stop the attack. As we said, while chivalry was existent at this time, that went away very quickly as Boelcke mandated that a combatant that was appearing to be going down still must receive attacks. This continuing attack was to ensure that the enemy was not using the guise of a false vi, or as it is said out west, "playing possum", as a means of escaping. If the enemy escapes, they may return to the fight and kill you, or worse, one of your fellow fliers.

If you look at the predator world you can see that a lioness, when possible, will preferably grab the throat of a gazelle and clamp down on the throat, crushing and collapsing the gazelle's windpipe and blood supply to the brain. You will also notice that the lioness does not stop this terminal attack for some time, even after the gazelle has stopped moving. Its goal is to ensure that their victim is dead. If it doesn't make sure the animal is dead, stopping the attack could mean the blood supply returns back to the gazelle's brain and it scurries off to safety.

Human predators will employ the same technique as the lioness to guarantee a kill. They will use as much violence as necessary to garner their resource. Any amount of resistance to their predatory behavior will be met with a disproportionate amount of violence to ensure the predator gets what they want. Simply put, this is not a quid pro quo. Instead, it is 'you do this, and I will up the ante even more'. Now what goes through the predator's mind is exactly what item number two in the Dicta mandates, get complete and utter dominance and follow through precisely to ensure that you get what you want, which in the German pilot's case was a dead enemy pilot. In the case of Gary Ridgway, the Green River killer responsible for at least seventy-one deaths of Seattle area women, it was about perverse sexual gratification, complete and utter dominance of another human being, then erasing the witness of his behavior. His attack was always continued.

The assumption of a kill or a victory is a fool's game, and efficient predators in the wild or the human world don't stop until the job is done.

The killing of the Russian mad monk Grigori Rasputin is legend, and a great story of follow through. As the story goes, Rasputin was lured into a cellar and fed cakes that were laden with poison, cyanide to be exact. The amount of cyanide was said to be five times the amount needed to kill a grown man. The assassins waited for the poison to take its toll and seeing no results, he was shot in the back and left to die. The assassins left the building, but one had forgotten his coat and returned to get it. As he entered the cellar, Rasputin awoke and attacked the young assassin by choking him. After a struggle, several other co-assassins appeared and shot Rasputin again. Standing over the fallen body of Rasputin the assassins discovered he was still alive because Rasputin was attempting to get up off the floor! In an effort to finally kill the mad monk, they clubbed him to death. Taking a page from the Mafia, before the Mafia was famous for this act, they then rolled Rasputin in carpet and threw him in the river. The autopsy of Rasputin showed that he had drowned. Poisoned, shot four times, bludgeoned, and finally drowned, you can see why skilled predators follow through with their acts of violence.

Number Three: Open fire only at close range.

As we said earlier, distance is your friend. Make potential attackers cross distance and act it in the light. Attackers want proximity, and they will use many methods to gain it; you in turn are not going to allow proximity.

Number Four: You should always keep your eye on your opponent.

We want to add another layer to your drills. What we want you to do is, once you have acquired the person that you are going to use for this drill, keep your eye on them. Here is the most common mistake that people make, once they have passed what they perceive to be a threat they shift their attention to the next thing in front of them. Another way to look at this is, "Since I can no longer see them they're no longer a threat." But as we have learned predators prefer to attack from the rear. It is beneficial to do a quick head check to make sure that they have not doubled back and in fact are attacking from the rear like any opportunistic predator or World War I ace. A straight-forward enough concept, and an essential one.

Number Five: In any type of attack it is essential to assail your opponent from behind.

It is important to include this even though we have stated in at least 100 different ways in this document that it is essential to "guard your six." By this time we've all become familiar with the idea of a blind spot and all the disadvantages this has for the victim as well as all the advantages it has for the predator. There is a nuance that is sometimes overlooked and it is, if the attack

If you don't see it coming, you're easy.

becomes linear, the attacker can attack in a straight line into the backside of the victim. The predator has already established that they believe that they can win because the victim is unaware and most likely slower, i.e., they do not possess the same attributes that the predator possesses. And the slower, less-skilled victim will most likely run in a straight line, allowing the predator to move in a straight line as well. Take a moment and think of it like a World War I ace. He would like to come out of the sun from a higher position and would like to be lined up with his opponent to shoot in a straight line into the length of their aircraft. This behavior gives what we call a linear track and linear response. This reduces options and simplifies the entire process for the predator

Number Six: If your opponent dives on you, do not try to get around his attack but fly to meet it.

This seems pretty simple, but let's break it down because in some instances, it is counter intuitive. What Boelcke is saying here is that fleeing from an attacker falls right in line with all of the advantages that they have as an attacker (see item Number Five). There is no advantage in initially trying to flee because it's too late. You are engaged, and trying to flee simply presents your six o'clock to the advancing predator, precisely what they would like. Let us be clear. We are not suggesting that you have to stand and fight. What we're suggesting is, if you have been engaged in an attack, it is too late and initially trying to flee will not be successful. You must engage the opponent at some level before you can secure a successful escape. Again, we want to be abundantly clear we are advocating keeping distance from the predator. However, what we are also saying is if there has been a closing of

Something to learn from the way of the rat. A cornered rat fights with everything it has.

distance and there is contact with the predator, turning and giving a return attack will aid you in securing an exit. Simply fleeing will present the weakest aspect of your defense to your attacker. Again, we cannot be more explicit than that this is a very narrow section of the continuum of violence. To drop back into the animal world for a moment, think of a cornered rat. We all understand the concept of a cornered rat. Rats will fight until the end of their life or until they can secure an escape. It can be expensive, so to speak, to go after a cornered rat.

Number Seven: When over enemy lines, always know your escape route.

Change the concept from enemy lines to unfamiliar territory. For example, let's say that you have traveled to another team's football stadium to watch your kid play football. You pull into the parking lot, park, and then go into the stadium. The question that we want you to ask yourself is, "How many routes of escape do I have out of here?" "Is there more than one entrance and exit to the stadium parking lot?" "I entered through gate 23, but is that the fastest way out of the stadium?" Wilder gives an example, "I go to Century Link Field for several football games a year. I am not always sitting in the same seats, so I'm always looking for the alternate routes out of the stadium should anything happen. Further, the way that they route me into the stadium is not necessarily the best escape. Instead of turning around and going back up the stairs and out the gate that they brought me in, it is better for me to run three rows forward, jump over the rail into a more expensive seating area and exit through that tunnel. Century Link Field's idea of crowd management has nothing to do with me devising multiple methods of exit."

We suggest finding the natural way, and finding multiple natural ways out of an unfamiliar situation. Nature always has multiple ways of solving problems. You should also establish multiple ways of solving your exit from a new, unusual area (or as Boelcke would put it, "Enemy Territory").

Number Eight: Tips for squadrons: in principle it is better to attack in groups of four or six. Avoid aircraft attacking the same opponent.

What is being expressed here is a division of resources, a good use of power to avoid having an uncovered opponent. This also removes the possibility of an accident, a pilot possibly killing one of his own in the confusion. Pack animals do the opposite as they bring the entire pack to the weakest point to kill the the target as quickly as possible. This works for pack animals as no weapon is involved. So both are saying and doing similar things - attacking in a pack, yet distributing resource when contact is made.

"I Chose You" Drill

Several times during the day choose somebody that you are not going to allow to come within striking distance of you. What is striking distance? The Tueller Drill is what we consider being striking distance. Whoever you chose you need to adroitly and with no observable effort keep them at the prescribed 21-foot distance. The person can be on the sidewalk, at your place of work, at a gymnasium or a sporting event. You choose the person and keep them at Tueller Drill distance. And we're going to tell you that you <u>have</u> to be very cool about it; don't be weird, don't give any clues that you are keeping this person at bay. Use your peripheral vision, don't necessarily make eye contact. Simply use this as a drill. This will help you learn how to move effectively through crowds, building habits in regard to keeping distance and game skills that you are drilling into your behavior.

The Clock Principle

As mentioned earlier, the Clock Principle is a simple method of establishing the orientation of an attacker in relation to the subject. Used by fighter pilots, the principle is this; straight ahead of you is 12 o'clock, directly behind you is 6 o'clock to your right 3 o'clock, to your left 9 o'clock and the rest of the numbers fill in about the clock. Seeming to be a victim, or having the mindset of somebody who's going to be attacked is not necessarily a way to go through life. As we discussed earlier animals use intermittent attention and groups to solve the problem of having to be on alert twenty-four a day, seven days a week. Further we would like you to become a strategic thinker instead of a tactical thinker. Think of it this way; using the coyotes as an example, coyotes will change their diet depending on the environment. If a coyote lives in Eastern Washington State its diet will consist of small mammals such as moles, rabbits, and insects. If a coyote lives in the suburban area where co-author Wilder lives in Seattle, you can add domestic cats to the coyote diet.

As you can see, adaptability to the environment is key. This is what predators do, they adapt. However, they are strategic thinkers, not necessarily tactical thinkers. We would like you to recognize that you too can be a strategic thinker instead of just a tactical thinker. However, part of this drill requires a couple of bullet points.

Exit Drill

The next supermarket, or store, you enter, find three ways of leaving the building if your initial path of entrance and exit should be blocked.

DRILL: Section 2 Continuation – Group

Here's a continuation of the drill from Section 2. Find a group in a crowd and choose to keep distance from them. One of the easiest groups to practice this drill with is teenage males. Teenage males make for great practice because they tend to cluster, which makes for easier observation. Teenage males also tend to be loud; they are busy demonstrating their prowess to their peers and engaging in loud brash behavior. As that cocktail of elements gets blended, they begin to respond like coyotes. A group of teenage boys becomes emboldened and willing to take risks and do things that they would not do solo. Coyotes will operate solo if hungry, or if a simple resource is easily obtained. But as a rule, coyotes find safety in numbers. With the ability and reason to act more boldly because of group support, teenage boys are identical to coyotes in this manner, and make for an easily visible subject for your avoidance drill. But we'd like to add a second aspect to this drill.

Once you have secured proper distance and have observed the group of teenage boys for a little bit, watch the ebb and flow of the social pecking order because this is identical to pack animals and their behaviors. This is your chance to watch low-end-resource pack predators and their behaviors. The key attribute of their aggressive behavior is exactly what Boelcke is recommending to his fighter pilots - attack in groups.

Eye Alignment

Most of the mammalian predators, including humans, of course, have eyes in the front of the face. But why is this? This is an important trait for being a successful hunter. Predators need stereoscopic vision.

Predators, in general have eyes facing forward for stereoscopic vision. Prey animals have eyes on the side for better peripheral vison. Guess where human eyes are.

If you think about it, creatures that hunt have to do an extreme unconscious calculation whenever they set up for, or pursue an attack. The main requirement for this is stereoscopic vision's main product, depth perception. Without it, the hunter cannot manage the complex muscular course corrections that bring it into physical contact with its prey. This results in misses, and enough misses means death and confirmation of Mr. Darwin's theories. It is very hard for predators in the natural world to long survive the loss of an eye.

Human predators don't have quite the needs of those in the animal world, but humans have been inflicting mayhem on each other for a very long time, and usually with some sort of force multiplier (weapon). Since the first proto human picked up a bone and cracked the skull of another proto human trying to take its food, we have been doing minute unconscious calculations of timing and distance to ensure impact or penetration.

What predators don't excel at is peripheral vision. A hunter's vision is designed to bring them into contact with their prey; a prey animal's vision is designed to prevent that very thing. Most prey animals have their eyes on the side of their heads. This "eyes on the side of the head" placement allows them to see more of the surrounding area and to scan for odd movements. However, many prey animals rely on their sense of smell or hearing more than their sight. Deer for example are fairly near sighted, often moving towards a still but suspicious shape, hoping for a sniff of scent or a sound that will identify the out of place item or animal.

While predators in the wild rely on a variety of senses, human ones generally rely on our main sense, sight. Because of this, it in our best interest to strengthen all our senses, as shown in a later exercise in this book.

Camouflaged

Standing at the McDonald's counter Wilder watched the group of teenage boys not being able to decide what to order and then changing their order several times, playing grab ass, not paying attention to those around them and other generally goofy behavior not uncommon for teenagers.

The attendant at the counter was becoming impatient with their behavior, and so was the elderly Asian woman standing directly in front of Wilder. A short African-American man in a red polo shirt also standing in line but off to the side he was triangulating Wilder and the elderly Asian lady. After a few minutes of frustration and fatigue the woman pulled up a chair and sat down waiting for the teenage boys to clear the area.

When the teenagers finally finished and shuffled off to the side of the counter, the African-American man looked at the elderly Asian lady in her chair and with his right hand palm upward, lifted his hand to his waist indicating, "It's your turn." Wilder looked at the man and gave an upward nod and a slight smile. The man looked back and offered no acknowledgment in any way; he simply looked back at Wilder motionless.

The teenagers began to engage in social jostling, tapping, pushing, and loud conversation. One of the teenagers, the tallest of the five or six, piped up with something very close to, "Don't mess with me, I'm a Blood," referring to the Los Angles- originated street gang. Wilder shrugged it off as teenage chatter and didn't take it seriously. However the African-American man, who moments ago offered the elderly Asian lady a place in line, heard what was said and he responded in an authoritative and clear voice, "Hey! You ain't no mother fuckin' blood." The teens' heads all snapped in the direction of the expletive. The tallest teenager quipped back, "Am too!" The same response, or lack of response, that was given to Wilder just moments ago was now bearing down in all its void on the tall teen. "I'm a Blood, "insisted the teenager again. The man didn't acknowledge the comment. The teen went on about how he knew the African American man in the red polo shirt, the significance of the color of the shirt now unveiled through the context of the interaction. The man stepped forward, paused and asked, "What's your name?" The teen responded happily in anticipation of recognition and acceptance. The young man continued to add more, talking out of nervous awkwardness about what kind of car the other guy was driving and where they had been "rollin.'" The man in the red polo shirt paused again for several seconds, during which time the gaggle of teenage boys remained utterly silent. "Yeah, I remember you now." Now validated each teen's body language begin to relax. The man in the red polo shirt, now clearly identifiable as a Blood, followed up with, "Yeah, I remember you ---you owe me fifty bucks." The body language of the group instantly changed to apprehension. "Outside." the Blood said. "What? No, I don't owe you fifty!" the teen replied. "Outside!" the Blood replied. The teen started walking toward the south door all the while protesting about the fifty dollars. The Blood said nothing. Wilder took the opportunity to leave the restaurant by the opposite north door. Circling around the parking lot Wilder got in his car and left. The next day a shooting was reported at that restaurant parking lot. No one died, just a bullet in the leg of a young man. The reason listed in the media was "a dispute."

Predators use camouflage, and they are dangerous. The Blood is this instance used the simple strategy of looking like something other than what he was. He had no obvious tattoos. No visible weapons. In a polo shirt and blue jeans the man looked like he was picking up a quick meal so he could get home and watch the game.

There are seven main forms of camouflage, depending on how you define them. It is rare that one animal will exercise only one of these seven means of deception. There can be overlaps, and there can be replacements to a methodology that doesn't work. Squid may attempt to threaten with multiple color changes and upon failure mute its tones and flee. The types of camouflage include:

Look like something else.

Clearly in this instance the Blood didn't look like a gangster. He looked like, well, just a guy. His pants and shoes said nothing special about him, but the red shirt told you everything you needed to know when the gang member chose to be known.

This is one of nature's primary means of camouflage, to look like something other than what you are. A great example of looking like something other than what you are is again the peacock. The peacock is not as physically as large as it appears to be when it expands its tail, and it only has two eyes compared to the multiple fake eyes that it has on its tail. With its tail unfurled, it appears as a true monster of fierce proportions with multiple eyes and much larger than the proposed attacker.

Break up your edges

Many reptiles are excellent at breaking up the edges; think the rattlesnake. The rattlesnake's coloring is similar to the ground and topography, the shapes and color of the area in which it lives. The designs in the skin of the rattlesnake break up the edges of the snake, allowing the snake to merge with the surrounding area. The shapes on the snake's skin, although rhythmic in its pattern, actually blend. Pattern is used by predators to seek out a resource, movement and shape being the two largest aspects of their protocols in the decision to attack or not attack. The diamondback rattlesnake has its pattern in its very name and is able to use the diamond pattern to hide in its environment. Ted Bundy, one of the United States' most prolific and famous serial killers, blended into the surrounding environment like the diamondback rattlesnake. Bundy was good looking, but crime is ugly, right? He studied law, was smart and career-oriented, but criminals are unemployed and shifty, yes? Ted Bundy, like the diamondback, was a deadly animal able to hide in plain sight.

Take away shadows

By staying in the shadows, and being dark you take away shadows. Shadows give depth; depth allows you to ascertain size and distance. Think of the black panther. This big cat prefers to hunt from above the eye line and to live in the shadows of the tree limbs. Human predators use the same technique, a dark hoodie and stand in the shadows.

Copy Cat

Animals use copycat behavior, or mimicry to stave off attacks. The theory works this way, "If I look like my attacker – hair, clothing, etc. – he may not attack me." This behavior makes the attacker pause to question the success of an attack. And this pause may well provide the opportunity to leave the kill zone unharmed. Mimicry is also used in a similar fashion in passive ways by insects that look like leaves, reptiles that look like venomous counterparts, or birds that are not raptors but have the markings of a hawk. Humans, as a military sniper can demonstrate, can, with the proper clothing and an understanding of the surrounding environment, mimic their surroundings and disappear. It is hard for a person to look like a leaf, or a bus seat, but they can look like something else other than what they are. A Shaolin monk looks like a monk yet their fighting prowess is legend.

Snipers attack from concealment for the most
successful results. So do most predators.

Multiple Tones

A squid is an example of an animal using multiple tones of color to
display, threat, camouflage, and desire to mate. It is all there in their

chromatophores, the cells
that allow an enormous variation in pattern and color.
Humans use multiple tones
as well, but it is the voice is
the natural tool of multiple
tones. Often inflection and
tone are more important than
the actual words spoken. Ask
anybody who has had a sar-
castic e-mail misinterpreted.

Chapter Eight
The Art of Awareness

Sense Meditation Drill

To learn to be more attentive to the changes that happen around you, you must learn to master the chattering monkey that most of us use for a conscious mind. Our logical mind was once intended as a tool, a supercomputer designed to solve problems that confronted us. The logical mind, which was intended for figuring out things so that our clawless, weak-toothed ancestors could survive, has taken over as we have evolved and now demands our constant attention. It is the authors' opinion that this function of the brain has been more than instrumental in building the Type A personality, the 'got so many things to do' mentality that is so pervasive today. The brain is like a rather spoiled child that can't sit still and constantly demands to be entertained.

One of the things that martial artists are reputed to develop is extraordinary awareness in their surroundings. Unfortunately, most only develop this awareness marginally at best, placing them just slightly above the average person in their ability to see the world. Much of the special senses that we see in martial artists in the movies do not exist. They are exaggeration, if not pure fiction, because we hardly take any time to train our senses This may be because we have never been exposed to ways of improving our perceptive abilities, and don't feel a need in the modern environment to develop these skills.

Find a sit spot.

This and the following training method are very loosely based on teachings from the Wilderness Awareness School's Kamana Naturalist Training Program. To do this, it is best to find a spot outdoors, that doesn't compromise safety, but will allow your senses to interact with the world. A back yard is fine and you should try to find a place where you can be both comfortable and unobtrusive. This is a spot you can visit regularly, and the more you do it the greater the reward. You could also pick someplace in the forest. For our needs a park bench, a back yard or almost any place you can sit for an extended time will work fine. (Someplace where you won't be bothered) Two important aspects of this site will be that it is handy and easy to access. Handy means you will use the site, and secondly it is in an area you frequent and as such you are highly familiar with it. We really want to underscore the importance

*It may seem odd that just sitting can increase awareness, but if practiced regularly, you teach **yourself** to listen and see.*

of the site being unobtrusive, easy for you to blend into. Returning to this spot and just observing as life moves around you can be a very rewarding experience, but the point of this is not just observation, but sharpening your senses and awareness.

Exercise 4: Five Sense Meditations

You may be familiar with different forms of meditation. Some forms are very divergent from others; some are similar even though their origins may be different.

When most of us think of meditation we think of monks or yogis sitting in uncomfortable positions and trying to keep thoughts from entering their minds while they look inward. While there is much to be gained from this, especially quieting the conscious mind and shutting out the distracting world, what we are doing in this exercise is precisely the opposite. We are seeking that distracting world in a direct and yet soft manner. Your intent is to focus on the distracting world so intently that it begins to show itself to you in a way that it has not in the past. One way to think of it is a form of ambient hyper vigilance. Try not to not make assumptions as to what will be seen. Be open to what comes.

Here is an example. Go to a park and listen to the sounds, the human sounds. One human sound is the sound of a car audio system. Listen to the music; is it aggressive? What does that music say about the person that selected the music? Young, full of testosterone? Is the music in effect an auditory marking of a territory? Or is it the greatest hits from the '70s, implying the person might be older, less interested in marking territory and more interested in revisiting younger days? You can see that simple observation can bring forth a wealth of information. With careful listening, you can tell a lot about the origin, the intent, and, using the Doppler shift and volume you can tell if the source of the music is coming your way or moving away.

Are the birds you are hearing agitated or calling for a mate? The only way you will know is to be open to the sound, become familiar with the sound, and using the experience you are gaining make an assessment as to what is being conveyed and what might be happening.

Our senses in the modern world have been blunted in a self-defense action against a day-to-day existence that is filled with things that demand our attention. The modern world is composed of things that might have had our primitive ancestors running in terror or curled up in the fetal position. To take on the task of opening our perception to a higher degree is not the place of the timid or the lazy; it takes effort. However, as the saying goes, fortune favors the bold.

The first protocol is for our vision. This seems almost superfluous. Sight is, after all, the main sense that human beings concentrate on, almost to the detriment of our other senses. But there is looking, and there is seeing.

Close Vision

Sitting in your sit spot, look straight ahead. Notice something close, it could be a flower, the grass, a garbage can, or a tricycle, just really look at it closely. This is a disciplined exercise, and your first inclination after looking at the object will be to assume you are done, as you have looked at it. This is where you can take a step outside of yourself and watch your chattering monkey mind demand to be entertained. Go back and look again. Draw the item into your mind, noticing the textures and colors. Everything in our existence affects everything

else, so how has the environment affected what you are observing? Is the flower young or old? What caused that garbage can to be so scratched up on that one side? Has that tricycle had an effect on the area? Ask yourself questions! How has the thing you are observing affected the flow of things around it? Now, look even closer.

Tracker Tom Brown Jr. has his students get down on their bellies in most of his early classes and observe things very close up. In the first class, people will follow vole (small hamster-like rodents) runs, dissecting trails, and finding vole hairs (about a half inch in length). After that class, it is almost impossible for students to cross a grassy field and not notice the runs and burrows of voles. In his second class he does the same thing with fox tracks. Thus, beginning trackers are born.

Here is an example. Over the course of a couple of weeks, about an hour before karate class, Wilder would cross the street to the library on the opposite side of the street from his dojo. There on the steps of the library Wilder would focus on the trees that were adjacent to the dojo. As the traffic light stopped and started traffic he would slowly gain the skill to ignore the rhythm of the cars and focus on the trees, then over time, one tree, and then one branch. The goal was to find one leaf and watch the leaf move in the breeze. Did the leaf have a rhythm as it fluttered in the wind? Did it touch other leaves? Was its color uniform?

The goal here is developing close vision.

This drill will become easier over time. It will become easier and quicker to have the experience of close vision. It takes, like we said, discipline and focus.

Now, try switching gears from using your central vision (where most of our attention focuses) to peripheral vision. Our side vision was once very important to our survival, but in this modern age, with so much of our attention drawn to what is right in front of us, (think computer screens or even small engine repair), our peripheral vision, because it is no longer critical is for the most part ignored.

First, let the focus of your main vision (center) go soft, then mentally force yourself to concentrate on what you see on each side. You're not turning off your center vision as much as you are just moving your attention to a wider, more encompassing field of vision. For humans, the process of using peripheral vision is; first, we catch something in the less clear area to our sides, then, we move our eyes and head to zoom in. We want you to ignore that response for now. Just watch with your less acute side vision, and see what motion, or detail, you can pick up. See how much you can make out before you turn and give it your full forward visual attention.

You need to know that you are not training your eyes; you are training your attention. This is also a great thing to try when out in a natural setting. The side vision is very good for picking up motion, and combined with a very slow pace can enable a person to see wildlife they would normally miss.

Hearing

One of our most-used senses is that of hearing. You go to sleep and you shut your eyes, you do not taste food while you sleep, but even

Training your hearing to 'hear deeper'.

though your mind chooses to ignore much of what it hears at night, the eardrum and adjacent parts are still working. Hearing is a sense that we can make large strides forward in increasing awareness of our surrounding environment.

For this exercise, first try to cut off our two major senses. Close your eyes tightly, cover your ears the best you can, and just sit for a minute or two with your heartbeat in your ears. Now, keeping your eyes tightly closed, take your hands away from your ears and just listen.

Maybe the first thing you'll hear is traffic. Ask yourself what direction is it in; how fast does it seem to be going? Then, listen deeper. Do you hear any human voices? How close are they? Are they male or female? How old are they? What is their emotional state?

Go a little deeper. Can you hear the birds? Do they sound like they're just singing regularly? Do they sound agitated? Have these noises always been there or are they just now starting to exist in this world (you know the answer to that), and why have you not noticed? Don't feel bad. As stated earlier, most of us aren't paying attention most of the time.

Do you hear anything walking across the grass? Most of us would not expect to hear a squirrel hop or a cat tread lightly by, but when you actually listen these things are perfectly normal. The naturalist Laurens Van Der Post said that if you listen intently enough in a very quiet place at night you can actually hear the ringing melody of the stars.

Taste and smell

The training of taste and smell is very similar; in fact, the tongue is part of the system of smell. For this drill sit with eyes closed and take long, slow breaths, in and out, using your nose. Tuck the tip of your tongue against the roof of your mouth and... smell. The strongest smells will come first,

With practice, your sense of smell can learn subtle nuance.

the garbage can or car exhaust from the street, but eventually the smell of grass will start to come though. Can you smell the cat or dog next door? Any laundry being done? A clothes dyer running? What trees and flowers are in the yard? Can you locate them without opening your eyes? You will experience some level of success quickly. Spending time with this drill will increase your skill and speed in short order.

Touch

The last part of this exercise is touch. Now you would think that there really isn't much to be gained by concentrating on our largest sense organ, our skin, but as we have demonstrated there is more here than meets general expectation. The sense of touch is pretty much an automatic response so why would we need to train it? Some believe that we sense more than the physical through our skin, that we can also sense the currents of energy around us. Plants and animals have energetic fields, but most of us, even when we feel this push against us, we rarely make that connection. We ignore a lot of what our skin feels.

Everything exudes energy. You can learn to feel it if you're willing to try.

There are many martial teachers who believe that human intent can be felt through the skin and translated into the nervous system. Surely everyone has had the experience of looking right at someone who was staring at you. In fact, many tests have been performed over the last 100 years to ascertain the validity of the ability of a person to sense being stared at by another person. The native peoples often warned young hunters about being too intent on an animal, staring at it and thus warning it, without physical stimuli, that it was being stalked.

Some would argue that the tingling sensation that they are feeling when being stared at takes place in the skin, and that is how it comes to conscious awareness. To explore this more you may want to follow the work of Rupert Sheldrake via his book: A New Science of Life: The Hypothesis of Morphic Resonance.

To improve touch, you need to spend some time concentrating on it. Sit in your spot and try running your hand over various plants. From some you may not get anything, from others, you may feel warmth or a tingling sensation. You can feel the energetic fields around the plants if you try. Clint has had great results with the plant Oplopanax horridus, commonly known as Devil's Club. Try a handrail, or a door as well, can you tell the difference with these objects versus plants and trees? If you can, note the difference, as it will be valuable for you in the future in discerning objects.

Two Person Drill

Using a trusted friend, relative or spouse, sit opposite one other in simple chairs. Sit closely yet not touching. Place your hands on your thighs and close your eyes. Now with your eyes closed have your partner project one strong emotion at you. Do you feel anything? Get a shiver down your spine? If not, don't feel bad. Many people spend years trying to train this skill, while others seem to be born with a sensitivity to this energy.

In the end, this is not just a chance to reacquaint yourself with your own senses. By enhancing your senses through practice, you enhance your autonomic awareness and your ability to notice when your body and subconscious are trying to tell you something. When this ability is in effect, you have to spend less time in "shivering Chihuahua" awareness.

Conclusion
Living Beyond the Level of the Obvious
– Tracks and Trails.

"Appearances are a glimpse of the unseen."

- Anaxagoras

The title of this final section is a misnomer for all the reasons you already know. You are now focusing on the obvious using the metaphor of the animal world – the obvious trails, actions and behaviors of human predators that are the telltale precursors to a violent action.

We have been conditioned to ignore these tracks, trails and behaviors. Further, we have bought into social procedures that make people say things such as, "He was just getting his life together" when a young criminal with a history of crime is killed in a violent act. Upon a review of their behavior, the trail they left behind, it is hard to come to a conclusion other than the violent end they experienced. Is it wrong to point to these incidents and say, "That is a sad ending"? No, but it is also important not to ignore the scope of that person's life, and we should add the concluding thought, "How else would it end?"

New skills are always a challenge. You will make errors in observation and in decisions. We make errors daily, but your goal should be to make those errors as small as possible, and to grow in your abilities of observation. As we move through life, regular observation of what is happening at this moment is what we should aspire to.

It is our sincere hope that we have reshaped the world you see; that you will, through the protocols, drills, stories, and lessons from the animal world use your new-found skills to remain safe, protect your loved ones, and live a very healthy, rich and wonderful life.

May the Awareness be with you.

Bibliography

The Kamana Naturalist Training Program
www.wildernesswareness.org
Author: Jon Young

Tom Brown's Field Guide to Nature Observation and Tracking
Author: Tom Brown Jr.
ISBN-10: 0425099660

What the Robin Knows
Author: Jon Young
ISBN-10: 054400230X

Facing Violence: Preparing for the Unexpected
Rory Miller
ISBN-10: 1594392137

Morphic Resonance: The Nature of Formative Causation
Rupert Sheldrake
ISBN-10: 1594773173

Other books by Kris Wilder

The Little Black Book of Violence:
What Every Young Man Needs to Know About Fighting
with Lt. Col. John R. Finch, Lawrence A. Kane and Marc "Animal" MacYoung

The Way of Sanchin Kata: The Application of Power

Dirty Ground: The Tricky Space Between Sport and Combat
With Lawrence A. Kane, Erik McCray and Marc MacYoung

The Way to Black Belt: A Comprehensive Guide to Rapid,
Rock-Solid Results
With Lawrence A. Kane

The Way of Kata: A Comprehensive Guide for
Deciphering Martial Applications
With Lawrence A. Kane and Dan Anderson

How to Win a Fight: A Guide to Avoiding and Surviving Violence
With Lawrence A. Kane

Lessons from the Dojo Floor

Other books by Clint Hollingsworth

Wandering Ones: Ghost Wind
Wandering Ones 2: Hawk Talon
Wandering Ones 3: The Mission
Wandering Ones: Scout Trail
The Art of Wandering (2015)